Celeste Longacre

Celeste's Garden Delights

Discover the many ways a garden can nurture you.

Understand that as you walk the Path that is your Life,

the Earth feels your footsteps.

She knows who you are.

This book is based on my own experience. It is not meant to be a complete treatise on any of these subjects. Use your own judgment when following the recipes. Remember, if it looks bad, smells bad or tastes bad, **don't eat it!** When in doubt, throw it out.

Also—everybody is different. While we share many nutritional needs, our ancestries and genetics can be different. We need to learn to listen to our bodies. Our guts speak to us whether through indigestion, aches and pains, cramps, irregularity or other symptoms. If something we eat bothers us, we should immediately discontinue its use.

Copyright ©2015 Celeste Longacre
http://celestelongacre.com/
ISBN 978-0-9916536-0-7 (Paperback)
978-0-9916536-1-4 (eBook)
978-0-9916536-2-1 (Kindle)

Dedication

To Bob, my husband and best friend,

who encouraged me to reach for the stars.

Acknowledgements

There are several people without whom this book would not have been possible. In addition to those interviewed in the "Other Voices" section, I would like to thank:

Erin Heidorn—for her stellar editing.

Garth Bacon and Ayla Joyce—for begging me to write this book.

Kay Hansen—for research.

Tom Stier—for cover design and layout.

Winslow Eliot—for publishing support.

Chefs Wesley Babb and Billy Boudreau—for their squash blossom recipes.

And friends and family for their continuing love and support, including Bob, Crystal Longacre Foley, Dan Foley, Madelyn Foley, Sasha Salzberg, Evan Carroll, Jesse Carroll, Silas Sonny Carroll, Bogart Salzberg, Ava Moskin and Sam Mosberg.

Table of Contents

Chapter One

Introduction

You've heard it: You are what you eat. The evidence is mounting that what you put into your mouth matters. What better way is there to take control of this truth than to grow some of your own food or get to know your farmer?

You can do it! This book will show you how to grow, can, ferment, freeze, dry and root cellar fresh produce. If you can't do it all, just do what you can. Start small. Do one thing differently this week and another next week. As you get used to the changes, they become completely natural and habitual. The benefits pay off not only in greater health but also in taste. Homegrown and homemade food (or locally grown and made) is far superior to anything that comes in a box. There's nothing like taking out a jar of garden delight (photo on cover) in the winter to warm your body and soul.

> As you get used to the changes, they become completely natural and habitual.

Even if you live in an apartment, you can grow a tomato or two in pots on the balcony or patio. Or, you can take a few hours in the summer to buy and prepare berries or corn for your freezer (it only takes four hours to freeze enough sweet corn to add to your soups and stews all winter long). It doesn't take a lot of time or effort to stock the pantry with some goodies.

Freezers are especially efficient these days. It actually costs very little to run a full-size freezer all year long. If you want to place it on the porch or in an outbuilding, just make sure that it is not a frost-free one.

If you have a lawn and would like to make part of it into a garden, the chapter on No-Till Gardening will tell you how to do it. Thinking about keeping chickens? Read the chapter on Backyard Chickens to see if it's something you really want to do. Want to experience rural life personally? Maybe a farmstay is right for you (see Other Voices section with Jackie Caserta).

Food is always less expensive when it is in season. Get together with some friends to take advantage of bulk buying. Farmers will usually give you good discounts if you buy large quantities or "seconds" (perhaps with a few bruises). If you don't live near a farm, spend a free day driving into the country with friends. Call ahead to see what is in season and what kind of deals are available. It's not difficult; it just has to be timely. In general, some kind of vegetable or fruit is in season from May through October (although citrus growers aim for December through March). Snap it up!

You can do it! It just takes a little determination and thoughtfulness. And, there's no better feeling than having an actual relationship with your food. Homegrown and homemade food (or locally grown and made) is absolutely the best.

Chapter Two

Sustainability in the 21st Century

My husband, Bob, and I have been living a sustainable life for decades. We did it because we wanted to. We worked very hard to create an environment around ourselves that was organic, natural, non-polluting, minimally trash-generating and largely self-supporting. When we began our journey, few people were interested in growing vegetables or keeping chickens. Food was unbelievably cheap and life was easy.

Now, however, times have changed. Food is no longer cheap and we are seeing devastating consequences in our weather and atmosphere, possibly from our lack of concern with sustainability. All of a sudden, people are waking up to the fact that we MUST become more aware. Not everyone (actually very, very few people) is going to be able to do exactly what Bob and I have done, but we can all do our part in this new Dance

> ...we are seeing devastating consequences in our weather and atmosphere, possibly from our lack of concern with sustainability.

of Life. This book will begin with our journey but it will also contain ideas for suburbanites, apartment dwellers and city folks. Sustainability can actually be euphoric. One of my best friends calls our place Shangri-La. Let's see what we can all do together.

Shangri-La

Bob and I live on almost six acres in the woods of New Hampshire. We grow nearly all of our vegetables for the whole year in our backyard garden. We keep chickens in a shaded coop at the edge of the forest (these provide us with delicious eggs and, eventually, soup). We have solar panels which give us just about all of our electricity in the summer months and much of it at

other times of the year. We can, we freeze, we ferment, we dry and we store our vegetables in the root cellar to eat all year long. We gather rain water for our garden from one of our roofs (although we also have a nice, deep, pounded well with delicious water for our own needs). We have a lovely, big screen porch for the summer and a sweet little sunspace on the south end that helps to heat the house in the

spring and fall. In the winter, we heat the house with our own wood. And, we have no mortgage. How we have ended up in this lush, peaceful, healthy and largely stress-free environment is the purpose of this book. It's a long story, so we'll start at the beginning.

For some reason, I have always hated debt. The thought of the bank actually owning my home sends shivers up my spine. Bob feels the same way. When we met, he had already begun building an octagonal house down a path into the woods off of a rarely used road. It was clean, light, warm and inviting except there was no water pumping into it, no sink for drainage and it was quite far from the electric lines. But he owned it free and clear. This was a true delight for me—we were free to just be. We didn't have to pound the pavement looking for jobs to pay the rent. The money we did make we could spend on whatever we liked. We agreed that we would get the amenities when we could afford to buy them.

We began by hauling water in from his brother's and friends' houses. Initially, we had to haul it out, too, but the first summer we were here, Bob created a grey water system to handle the used water and installed a kitchen sink. We had a woodstove to keep us warm and a gas propane stove for cooking. Kerosene lamps provided light in the evenings and the water we hauled could be heated by either of the stoves. We joined the local YMCA for showers.

We can, we freeze, we ferment, we dry and we store our vegetables in the root cellar to eat all year long.

After three years, we put in a well and installed a hand pump at the kitchen sink. I felt like I had moved into the Hilton! Water flowing right into the house! It was an absolute joy. We had a small black and white television that we ran off of a car battery. Every Friday I would bring it into town and a gas station would charge it for me (they called me the battery lady). We gave our daughter, Crystal, baths in a big washtub which we placed right next to the woodstove in the winter. We warmed up her towels by holding them next to the woodstove before she got out. We bought shower bags that hung in the Sun in the summer and took showers outside. We bought a generator so we could more easily keep the house tidy with a vacuum cleaner and, eventually, got a computer that we ran off of one solar panel on our roof. It was important to remember to fill the globes of the kerosene lights and trim the wicks daily before it got dark. We kept water heating on the woodstove all winter long.

> Our life had more chores than most folks, but we still had no debt. And, we were active and healthy. We were happy.

Our life had more chores than most folks, but we still had no debt. And, we were active and healthy. We were happy.

Then one day, eleven years after I had moved into the octagon, my computer refused to work. It had been a cloudy stretch and there just wasn't enough juice in the battery. I was frustrated by this and immediately thought that it was time for us to join the grid. Bob was sleeping upstairs at the time and when he came down, said that he had just dreamed about two men cutting a path through the woods near our house with chainsaws. I said, "That's because it's time for us to get electricity." And he agreed.

The power lines were brought to the top of the hill, then we buried the last 400 feet. That way we didn't have to cut down the trees around our house; we enjoy being tucked in. A friend brought over his backhoe and we laid the pipe ourselves, even walking it through a casing to protect it. We had ordered the power in the spring, but it wasn't until November that the power company installed it. We live downhill from the poles and the very first bucket of dirt that came out of the ground hit water. The water followed us all the way down the hill. It was a cold, wet and extremely strenuous day but we got the power hooked up. Bob built an addition to house all the water-based appliances and we hired a plumber to hook them all up. We now had a water tank, water heater, tub, bathroom sink, kitchen sink and washing machine. We continued to use our outhouse so that we could remain on the grey water system. It took eleven years, but we had a nicely functioning house and we owned it!

The Garden

When I was twenty years old, I read Adelle Davis' "Let's Eat Right to Keep Fit." Her premise in this particular book was that—if you want to be

14

healthy—you have to pay attention to what you eat. Wow! This made so much sense to me. Our bodies need nutrients in order to build and repair their essential cells. Real food has been supplying these nutrients for hundreds of thousands of years. However, at the time I read this book, there was much for sale in the supermarket that was utterly and completely different from traditional "foods." Extruded cereals, processed chips, manufactured candies, sugary sodas and a plethora of items containing new "ingredients" filled the shelves. I definitely did not want to be eating these foods. So, I decided to become an organic consumer and to grow as much of my own produce as possible.

Building a proper garden took some work. The property that my husband had purchased was basically a sucker forest. This meant that the entire piece was covered with trees about two to three inches across, six to ten inches apart and ten feet tall. We picked an area to place the garden and went to work. Bob cut the trees and pulled the stumps and I pick-axed out the roots. We had a dump truck full of manure delivered to the property and let it sit for a year to cook out any bugs and weeds before we used it in the garden. Bob made raised beds out of green hemlock (we didn't want to use pressure-treated because it contains arsenic) and we were in business. Of course, the first year, the garden was about as big as a normal kitchen table. The second year

we doubled it and for several years continued to add beds until it was large enough for our needs. We used to have manure delivered every year. Today (over thirty years later) we get manure about every two years. There are now about thirty beds in the garden.

Unfortunately, our hemlock beds began to disintegrate after

He did the entire project with a shovel, a wheelbarrow and a piece of carpet (to aid in getting the stones into the wheelbarrow).

a few years. Bob would look out when the snow melted each spring and see lots of work to do. He would nail the boards together with brackets but they continued to look worse and worse each year. One day, about twenty years ago, he decided that he would redo the entire thing in stone. This was not a small project. He rummaged around the property looking for stone (they don't call New Hampshire the "Granite State" for nothing), piling it up for perusal. He needed two flat sides of the rocks for the beds but the other two sides were far from square. So it was like putting together a vast puzzle. He did the entire project with a shovel, a wheelbarrow and a piece of carpet (to aid in getting the stones into the wheelbarrow). He dug out the beds and fitted in the stones. He spent two or three days a week all summer long for seven years building me an absolutely gorgeous garden. When it was done, he asked me, "What would you like in the paths?" I answered, "Stone would be nice." So the next three years were involved with building the paths. I asked a friend with a nursery to grow me some creeping thyme to plant in between the stones and it slowly filled in these spaces. Now it truly looks like a European garden that's been there for centuries. And it is such a pleasant place to work!

The House

When I moved in, the house was a big octagon. Old rugs covered the plywood floor and the ceiling was an incessant repetition of Johns Manville Insulation. The first addition that we built was for a pantry. Since we didn't have electricity, I did a lot of canning on the gas stove and I needed a space to store my efforts. Originally, I purchased the tomatoes, peaches and other produce in season from local farmers. So Bob built me a nice room (the size of a medium walk-in closet) with shelves designed for quarts and pints and we experimented with a passive refrigerator under the floor. The space wasn't very big (maybe eighteen inches by two feet) but Bob shoveled dirt around the outside to earth-berm it and put a trap door in the floor of the pantry. Since we live in northern New England—a cold climate—it worked like a charm. July was a bit of a bust, but most of the rest of the year the passive refrigerator stayed cold and never froze.

July was a bit of a bust, but most of the rest of the year the passive refrigerator stayed cold and never froze.

Inspired, we decided to build a real root cellar under our next addition. Bob first built a small cellar (about four feet by six feet) out of cinder blocks coming right up to the joists that hold the floor. He also tied them into the floor framing so that rodents couldn't come in and then poured a cement floor. Again, he earth bermed the space before building the next addition. He built a downstairs space to hold his tools and a lovely "tower" (with a curved wall) upstairs for our daughter's bedroom. I probably should say "up-ladder" as we use inside ladders, not stairs, to get to the second floor. He finished her room with a beautiful wood ceiling and hardwood floor.

Bob tackled the octagon's ceiling next. Our bedroom loft covers only half of the available space so we have a nice, tall ceiling in the living room. We bought some eight-inch tongue and groove and shiplap pine and Bob spent several weeks nailing it over the insulation. I loved it. Looking up, I now saw only beauty.

The third addition was added when we anticipated the arrival of electricity and hot running water. Going ten feet outside of the kitchen wall, Bob built a beautiful space—complete with skylights—to hold all of our plumbing. It was truly a glorious day when all of the appliances were hooked up and working! I was absolutely thrilled to have hot running water at the mere turn of a faucet.

> I was absolutely thrilled to have hot running water at the mere turn of a faucet.

A Sustainable Diet

The human gut and digestive system have evolved over many thousands of years. Our immune systems have worked hard to identify and classify a checklist of "okay" items as they pass into our bloodstreams. Carrot? Yes, it's on the list! Beef? Yes, this too is on the list. I could go on with the many, many things that actually are on the list.

Today our immune systems are bombarded with many items that are NOT on the list: red 40 dye, blue 2 dye or yellow 5 dye? What should we do with these? High fructose corn syrup, aspartame, dimethylpolysiloxane, potassium benzoate or sodium tripolyphosphate? Definitely not on the list. So what does our immune system do with these items? They aren't used to nourish, maintain or heal our cells. Are they simply stored somewhere or excreted? Does anybody really know?

Many of our grandparents (or great grandparents) had a garden. Up until World War II it was simply a part of life to grow some of our own food. When someone bought hamburger, it generally came from a farm down the road where the cows ate grass, roamed about in the sunshine, spent winters in a roomy barn and were personally tended by a farmer. Veggies and fruits came from local orchards which were tended without pesticides, herbicides or petroleum-based fertilizers. These mini farms were quite diverse; many folks kept a few chickens and used their composted manure to fertilize beds of carrots, tomatoes, cucumbers, potatoes, squashes, beets and melons. Chemical fertilizers were unknown. Now it's a different story.

After World War II, things changed dramatically. Chemical fertilizers were introduced into the soil to replace traditional manures. So-called "conventional" vegetables were dosed with dozens of different toxic sprays and fed chemical fertilizers. Packaged foods appeared in the supermarket which were ready to eat and full of hard-to-pronounce and unfamiliar ingredients to preserve shelf life. Cows, pigs and chickens soon became warehoused in huge, unsanitary feedlots necessitating the use of antibiotics to keep the animals alive.

Cattle feedlots largely appeared in the 1950s and 1960s as a result of abundant grain harvests. Farmers learned that they could bring cattle into one location and fatten them up on corn to add lucrative weight before slaughter. Many of these cows spend all day in small, concrete pens where they can't move around and all of them have indigestion (cows aren't supposed to eat grains).

Pigs fare little better. Many spend their whole lives in a small cell located inside a barn. The air smells bad and their waste smells even worse. In a natural setting, pigs like to frolic in the woods digging up tubers and eating acorns.

Many chickens are now raised in huge barns, some of which can house 20,000 birds, and are stacked one row upon another in cages so small that they can't even totally open their wings. They never see the sunshine or get to eat greens or insects. Their conditions are so unsanitary that the farmers have to routinely give them antibiotics to keep diseases away.

I strongly believe that every living creature (plant or animal) carries with it the experiences it has lived. Could our skyrocketing depression rate be partly due to the fact that we consume extremely traumatized meat? Luckily small, local farms seem to be popping up all over the place. Young people are once again professing an interest in this occupation and they want to do it in a healthy way.

We definitely are what we eat. However, we are also made up of what our food eats.

We definitely are what we eat. However, we are also made up of what our food eats. Almost nothing in nature has 20,000 of anything (blueberries, robins, frogs, squirrels or foxes) in one place. A natural setting has a little bit of this and that with a smattering of an awful lot of other things. Old-fashioned farms have a cyclical sustainability about them. The grass feeds the cattle and the cow poop helps the grass to grow. Chickens eat the garden weeds and their poop (composted) aids the vegetables to thrive. Goats and pigs can be quite useful in clearing land as they love to forage plants that are nastily established on rolling hills and dales. We need to get back to this more natural way of vegetable farming, eating, composting and raising animals.

Our health has been terrifically jeopardized by this plethora of unnatural ingredients. Not only are they toxic to our systems but they take the place of food that would be able to truly nourish us. We need to get back to what nature intended—real food. Support your local farmers' market. Find the people in your area who are growing crops and raising livestock sustainably and shop there. Get to know your farmer.

Get to Know Your Farmer

Ideally, if you can't grow your own food, you should live as close to a farmer (or farmers) as possible. Luckily, farmers' markets are popping up all over the place these days so you probably won't have to travel far to partake in marvelous seasonal fruits and vegetables. When getting to know your farmer, ask if you can come and tour the farm (shop elsewhere if they say no). Organic is nice but lots of farmers who don't use chemicals are not registered as such. Ask what kind of fertilizers are used and if they spray for insects or weeds. Find out what's in season and what goodies will be coming next. Anyone, even an apartment dweller, can throw some blueberries in the freezer or can a few tomatoes.

> Organic is nice but lots of farmers who don't use chemicals are not registered as such.

Getting to know your local farmer also benefits your own garden. I have never met a farmer who isn't willing to chat with me about problems that I am experiencing. Since many of these difficulties are regional, the very best source of information comes from those who are also attempting to grow things where you are. Many farmers will take on apprentices and actually teach how to grow vegetables or raise animals. Small, local farms most likely offer us the healthiest food as they almost always have a great diversity of vegetables and their animals (hopefully) are treated to fresh air, sunshine and fields of grass. Again, ask if you can tour the farm to be sure.

> # Freezers don't actually require a lot of energy to maintain their coldness.

Farmers will often offer discounts if you want to purchase large quantities of an item. In many areas the growing season is short but abundant. Buying in bulk and freezing the extra food can save you some money. Freezers don't actually require a lot of energy to maintain their coldness. In cold climates, freezers can be kept in outbuildings or enclosed porches (if electricity is available) where they are virtually free to maintain in the winter months. However, if you are planning to use a freezer outside, remember that it can't be a frost-free freezer. These machines routinely heat up the insides to reduce the frost and will break in a very cold environment.

Supporting local farms also keeps your dollars in your own local areas. Never underestimate the power of your spending choices. If you must shop in supermarkets, ask the manager to carry local produce and meats.

> # Never underestimate the power of your spending choices.

Chapter Three

The Garden Plan

Gardens are always a work in progress. Each year, the weather is somewhat different. Insects that were previously unknown hitch a ride with neighbors' plants and migrate into your own backyard. Animals dig under fences and wreak havoc. So gardens need to be watched and tended to regularly.

One of the best ways to mitigate insect damage is to rotate crops (planting different crops in each bed from year to year). This is also a way to keep the plants healthy as individual vegetables will take varying amounts of nutrients out of the soil each year. It's essential to have a plan.

I use a three-year crop rotation plan. Four years would be better, but I don't have the space. By crop rotation, I mean that a family of vegetables only lives in a single bed once every three years. Plants actually have families, other crops that they are closely related to that share the same nutrient needs and pest infestations. By moving crops around, not only do you at least make it a little

> One of the best ways to mitigate insect damage is to rotate crops (planting different crops in each bed from year to year).

more difficult for the bugs to find their favorite food, but you also rest the beds from heavy feeding of one particular nutrient group.

The families are as follows:

Cruciferae: Includes all of the Brassicas—cabbage, broccoli, Brussels sprouts, cauliflower, kale, turnips, rutabaga, kohlrabi and radishes.

Solanaceae: Is often referred to as the nightshade or tobacco family. It includes tomatoes, potatoes, eggplants and peppers.

Cucurbitaceae: Includes cucumbers, squash, pumpkins, melons and gourds.

Umbelliferae: Includes carrots, parsnips, celery, parsley and dill.

Leguminosae: The pea or legume family which includes all the peas, beans, peanuts and clover.

Compositae: Most of the salad greens including lettuce, endive and chicory.

Chenopodiacease: Contains spinach, Swiss chard and beets.

Alliums: All of the onion-type vegetables including chives, shallots, leeks and garlic.

Seeds

Seeds are the beginning of life. While often infinitesimally small, they represent the potential for sustainability in the world of nourishment. Farmers—for thousands of years—have been painstakingly collecting, drying and storing seeds from one year to another.

Recently, however, large agribusiness has begun to grow, sell and promote seeds that either won't reproduce or have legally been patented so that the farmer is forbidden from collecting their seeds. This policy is completely anti-life. In a sustainable world, seed collection is a must. This is the only way that we can keep our agriculture going from one season to the next. We need to conscientiously avoid purchasing these patented, largely genetically-modified seeds and support the many local, organic seed companies that put no such

> **Seeds need to be carefully dried (away from the Sun) in order to remain viable.**

limits on their products. Or, we need to begin to harvest our own seeds.

If you want to collect your own seeds, you need to be a little stingy with your varieties. Bees don't differentiate a Brandywine tomato from a Black Russian and, if they taste and pollinate both, the seeds will be a combination of the two instead of a true single variety. So limit the varieties of the vegetables from which you'd like to collect seeds to one or plant different varieties very far apart (at least thirty feet). Also, F1 hybrid seeds will not reproduce a similar plant. They are bred to be unreproducible from themselves. These are generally seeds from two separate "parents" that need to be repurchased every year if you want the same variety.

Seeds need to be carefully dried (away from the Sun) in order to remain viable. After that, the most damaging thing for seeds is constant fluctuations of humidity. For this reason, I keep my seeds in large glass jars with tight lids. I buy most of my seeds (because my garden is relatively small and the different varieties are close together) and the moment I receive them, they go into glass jars. I also keep my unused seeds for five years even though I purchase new ones each year. Over time they lose their viability, even in the glass jars, but often a particular variety is unavailable to buy due to crop failure. This way, I can still plant my favorites although more seeds will need to be planted as fewer will germinate. This also represents a kind of "insurance" for me. Who is to say that these seeds will always be available?

There are many wonderful sources for buying seeds. The Seed Savers Exchange, Johnny's Selected Seeds, Seeds of Change, Territorial Seed Company, Fedco, Pinetree Garden Seeds, Vermont Bean Seed Company, Irish Eyes Garden Seeds, John Scheepers Kitchen Garden Seeds, Totally Tomatoes, Wood Prairie Farm, The Maine Potato Lady, The Cook's Garden and R.H. Shumway are just a few of my favorites.

Turn a Piece of Your Lawn into a No-Till Garden

Are you interested in having a garden but are not sure how to replace the green lawn you see outside your window? Have no fear! You can easily turn a piece of this lawn into a beautiful garden. However, it's most important to choose a proper location. Gardens have certain needs. Vegetables should have at least six hours of sunlight to produce their crops. So be sure that the place you'd like to garden isn't shaded by trees, the garage or the house for any significant part of the day (sometimes taking pictures throughout the day can help you to identify where this happens). You also don't want to locate it near a gutter drainpipe or where cars driving by in wet weather would splash up the contents of puddles. Look for it to be free of tree roots or other large plants that could steal the nutrients from your crops. Your garden will also need to be in a place where water can drain, so avoid areas that routinely have standing water for a day or two after a storm. It's best to be free of lawn chemicals or other pollutants.

> Your garden will also need to be in a place where water can drain, so avoid areas that routinely have standing water for a day or two after a storm.

And, there should be a water source nearby—you don't want to be hauling water long distances.

Take some time to develop a plan. It's best to start small. Choose the vegetables that you like the most—perhaps tomatoes, cucumbers, beans or summer squash. Read seed catalogues in order to learn the needs of the various plants. Some need to be staked, others need room to spread; plan accordingly. Figure that beds, ideally, are three to four feet wide.

Then, starting in the fall, gather the materials you are going to need to create your no-till garden: newspaper, rocks, cardboard, wood chips, dirt and lots of compost. The best way to get compost if you don't create it yourself is to find a local, organic farm. Farmers who have several cows, chickens, goats, sheep, pigs or llamas will often have large piles of old manure. They generally are able to sell it for a modest amount. Shop

Remember, you want to be able to reach the middle of each bed without stepping in it so don't make them too wide.

around. For a small garden, you could take a pickup truck and shovel the humus-rich material in and out yourself. For larger gardens, you may want the farmer to deliver it in a dump truck.

Pick a pleasant day to begin this adventure. Get friends or the kids to help. This is a slow process and it won't be accomplished in a few minutes so allow plenty of time. Mark off the perimeter of the bed (or beds). Remember, you want to be able to reach the middle of each bed without stepping in it so don't make them too wide. If you are dealing with a grassy area, you needn't do any mowing. However, if there is brushy stuff growing, take the time to cut it down to soil level. If you are going to have paths between your beds, make sure that they are wide enough for a wheelbarrow to fit through.

Newspapers now use soy inks which are more biodegradable than petroleum-based inks. Soak six to eight layers of newspapers (no glossy pages or magazines) in water for several hours. Place these on the ground in your marked-off area and layer thickly, making sure that they overlap so that grass will not find its way up through the cracks. Place a few rocks on top to keep the papers from blowing away. Next, add a layer of good, organic compost at least eight inches high on top of the newspaper. In addition to aged compost, grass clippings, mulch hay or non-acid leaves (like maple, ash or beech) can be used. Throw some dirt on top to hold it all down. Paths should be covered

> **When choosing plants, look for a good root system; ideally, the roots below the soil should equal the foliage above the soil.**

with cut and overlapped cardboard. Building supply stores and farm and garden shops often give plain, uncut cardboard away. Cover the cardboard with four to six inches of wood chips. Chips are often given away free from tree companies that are looking for a place to dump them, or can be purchased at feed stores or farm and garden shops. Once all your layers are in place, leave it be for the winter.

Come spring, this bed will be ready to plant. Put the seeds right on top and cover with a layer of compost or aged manure. You might want to add some organic alfalfa meal and kelp meal to give your plants an extra boost. Dig transplants right into the ground. Be sure that the seeds you are sowing as well as the transplants that you are using are disease-free. Buy from a local, reputable source. Beware of big box stores as their sources can import diseases or insects from other areas. When choosing plants, look for a good root system; ideally, the roots below the soil should equal the foliage above the soil.

> **The nutrients in the compost will get into your plants and, thus, into you.**

As the season progresses, it might be wise to continue layering organic compost to feed the plants. Mulch applied two or three times will help with moisture retention and will also keep the weeds down. Straw is generally not recommended as fields are often sprayed with pesticides before they are planted with straw. When choosing what to use in your garden, organic is always best. Be sure that you get not only organic seeds and transplants but organic soil amendments as well.

Once your bed is established, you will need to repeat the layering process of newspaper, compost, mulch and dirt each fall. In doing this, you are actually creating healthy soil. The nutrients in the compost will get into your plants and, thus, into you. The no-till system necessitates that you never turn your soil. Some believe that this is the truest form of gardening as it mimics nature; trees never rake away their leaves. The micronutrients that feed the plants remain intact as do the earthworms that aerate the soil without disturbance.

Protecting the garden from predators could require a garden fence, an electric fence or a buffer zone. Tall grasses allow animals to hide so it's best to keep the grass around the edges cut.

Planting in Pots

Many folks don't have big yards, especially if living in a condo or apartment. But, even if you just have a patio or balcony, you can plant some vegetables or flowers in pots. The principles are pretty much the same. Most vegetables and flowers need at least six hours of Sun, good organic soil, some supplements like kelp meal and plenty of water. Be sure that the container you choose has drainage at the bottom. Otherwise, a good rain storm could fill the pot up and drown the plant.

The most critical aspect of container gardening is to maintain the moisture level. Plants grown in pots tend to dry out much more quickly than those grown in garden soil. Some nurseries and garden catalogues sell self-watering devices which could

> Before adding the soil I always place an unbleached folded paper towel over the hole at the bottom. This ensures that the soil will stay in the pot while the moisture can still escape.

be essential if you plan to go away for a few days. Or, get friends to stop by to water your plants while you're away.

When planting in pots, I like to choose the largest container I can find that will fit in my space. Make sure it is clean (if it is a re-use, be sure to bleach it before using it). Before adding the soil I always place an unbleached folded paper towel over the hole at the bottom. This ensures that the soil will stay in the pot while the moisture can still escape.

It's a good idea to use the best potting soil you can. Purchasing all natural (without any chemicals or hard-to-pronounce additives) will help you grow the best quality plants. Seeds should be planted to a depth about twice their thickness. Ask your nursery about transplants; some plants have to be planted at the exact same level as you receive them while others, like tomatoes, can go as deep as you can get them.

Leave an inch or two of space between the height of the soil and the top of the rim. This will allow water to be caught by the plant when it rains or when you water it. Follow all the other recommendations for each type of plant you are growing (does it need to be staked or have room around it to spread out?). Good luck!

Chapter Four

My Year

I am sharing with you my yearly planting and harvesting cycle. It is, perhaps, true only for those of us who live in the northern part of this country (USA). Yet, it shows the importance of having a monthly plan. This basic structure can be amended to fit into any region—but it often takes several years to figure out what actually works best for you. To aid you, local nurseries can be quite helpful and most states have extension services with free tidbits for anyone who asks.

> This basic structure can be amended to fit into any region—but it often takes several years to figure out what actually works best for you.

January

While the snow remains on the frozen ground and I snuggle by the woodstove fire, this is the month to finalize the garden plan that I began in the fall. It's important to rotate crops; this makes it a bit more difficult for last year's bugs to find their favorite meal and also because dissimilar plant families draw separate minerals from the soil.

I peruse the seed catalogues thinking about what has worked well for me in the past and which new varieties I want to try. I always buy at least one new vegetable or variety to keep things interesting. Of course, there are my die-hard favorites and I want to be sure to purchase these before the seed companies run out of them (I actually sometimes buy my seeds in December for this reason). It's quite fun to look at ripe, red tomatoes and juicy cantaloupes when the world outside my window is nothing but white. When the seeds arrive, I immediately place the packages in large glass jars with tight lids. Nothing damages the viability of seeds more than changes in atmospheric moisture. These jars stay in a cool, dark place until planting time.

While part of me longs for the abundance of summer, another part is very content to sleep a lot and create wonderful meals from the larder. January is my time to catch up on reading, writing or sewing.

There are great local nurseries, though, which seem to do a better job growing them from seed than I can so I usually just buy my tomato plants from them.

February

This is the month that I start my onions. I dutifully take out my potting soil, trays and seeds and get to work putting them all together (see section on Onions in the Planting the Veggies chapter).

March

The days are getting longer and the temperature is beginning to warm some. If I was going to grow my own tomato plants from seed, I might start them indoors near the end of this month. There are great local nurseries, though, which seem to do a better job growing them from seed than I can so I usually just buy my tomato plants from them.

I keep an eye on the onions and double check my seed collection to make sure I have all that I will need. I also look to see if I have enough twine and I often begin cutting the strips of cotton for the tomatoes (see section on Tomatoes in the Planting the Veggies chapter). I try to get some extra sleep because next month the real work of the season begins.

April

The first thing that I want to get done in April is to clean the chicken coop. It's warmer now and the garden will soon be commanding all of my energy so I take care of the chickens while I have the time.

Lots of things can be planted outside now even though there will still be many frosty nights. I start with lettuce. After a month or more the leaves get bitter, so I actually plant it every couple of weeks all summer long. That way we can continuously eat the sweet, tender young plants. Next the peas go into the ground. Then I plant Brassicas—broccoli, cabbage and Brussels sprouts. Beets, parsnips, Swiss chard and turnips go in next. Towards the end of April, I transplant my onion plants into the garden. This work generally keeps me busy until May.

May

In early May, I buy some leek plants and transplant them into the garden. Dill is sown next. Sunflowers can now be planted as well as the first ten or so of my gladiola bulbs, calendula and potatoes. I will have to carefully watch the gladiolas and potatoes because their shoots are tender, but it generally takes a couple of weeks for them to appear and the frost should be done by then. In order to get my favorite varieties, I will often buy a few tomato plants early in the month and tuck them into my greenhouse. For someone without a greenhouse, these plants could be placed in a sunny window and brought outside for short periods of time on warm, sunny days. Before all the tomatoes go into the ground, they will have to be hardened off (brought outside for short, then longer periods of time on warm days). I start to eat the lettuce this month and it's lovely to have something fresh for a change. By late May, everything else needs to be planted. I generally wait until May 22 to plant the carrots (see Planting the Veggies section on Carrots for the explanation).

Memorial Day Weekend is a marathon for me. In go the tomatoes, sweet peppers, paprika peppers, pumpkins, summer squash, zucchini, butternut squash, statice, marigolds, basil, parsley, cosmos, snap dragons, more gladiolas, celery, green beans, cucumbers, eggplant, okra and sweet potatoes. I often try to get some help as it is a big job.

June

I've been thinning, weeding and watering the beds before now, but this month it begins in earnest. Every plant needs room to grow and I tend to sow rather thickly. The thinnings can go to the chickens (which they love). I also begin tying the tomato vines to their supports and looking for the asparagus beetle.

> Now I check plants every morning in June and knock the beetles into a container of water (when they see you coming, they run and hide behind the plants).

For ten years I didn't have any problems with the asparagus beetle and was taken by surprise when my plants suddenly began being eaten by them. Now I check the plants every morning in June and knock the beetles into a container of water (when they see you coming, they run and hide behind the plants). I used to put them into soapy water, but switched to plain water since I now feed them to the chickens.

The strawberries ripen in June so this is when I make strawberry-rhubarb jam.

July

This is the month that the Japanese beetle and the harlequin bug make an appearance. They can attack a variety of plants but in my garden they both seem to like my green beans, asparagus and roses best. I knock them into a container of water and feed them to the chickens. This is best done early in the morning or late in the evening when it is too cool for the beetles to fly. The asparagus beetle often also makes a reappearance this month.

> The thinning, weeding and watering continues and—as it gets hot—the watering becomes even more critical.

The thinning, weeding and watering continues and—as it gets hot—the watering becomes even more critical. Peas are harvestable early in the month and the green beans begin to ripen by the middle of the month. Also by mid-July, I start to check on the garlic. The garlic's many green leaves begin to die back and when there are only four left, it's time to harvest. Blueberries and broccoli begin to ripen in earnest this month and I spend quite a bit of time picking and freezing them.

Swiss chard is now ready to eat and beet and carrot thinnings are also becoming an edible size. Cucumbers are popping off their vines and sometimes the eggplant and okra are also ready. The zucchini and summer squash are delicious.

Basil, oregano, thyme, calendula and tarragon can now be dried. I don't personally grow corn, but I love to have it in my freezer. I buy it first thing in the morning from a local, organic grower and get it right into my freezer (see Planting the Veggies section on Corn). In my opinion, the very best corn is ready in late July or early August.

August

Now the garden is beginning to come alive. Tomatoes and peppers are finally ripening and it's time to make the cucumbers into pickles. The peppers and blackberries go into the freezer and the tomatoes are put into jars. Blackberry and crabapple jams are made. More broccoli and green beans also go into the freezer. Garlic is peeled, sliced and dried in preparation for making garlic powder.

> Onions are typically harvested the second week of August.

Onions are typically harvested the second week of August. After they come out, I plant a wintering-over spinach and lettuce in the now-empty space. By the end of the month, spaghetti sauce is created and canned. I often get the sand for the root cellar at the end of this month as well. It needs to be quite dry (and replaced every year).

September

With summer's end approaching, it's a race to get everything preserved. More tomatoes are canned into sauce and garden delight (a lovely mix of onions, peppers, tomatoes, basil, garlic, oregano and thyme—photo on cover). Pumpkins and butternut squash are picked and begin their sunning process (they need two weeks of Sun to toughen them up for storage). Beets, carrots, potatoes and turnips go into the root cellar. Grapes are made into jam.

I also begin to watch the weather for frosty nights. If frost threatens, I cover the lettuce, spinach and cabbage, or any beds of carrots or beets that haven't yet made it into the root cellar, with old sheets or Reemay®.

The garden clean-up is also at hand. By the end of this month, a frost is sure to have come so most of the beds need to be raked and freed of debris. I cook some compost to make my own potting soil for the onions and amaryllis (outside in a soil sterilizer), bringing it up to 200°F to eliminate any bugs or diseases. This soil gets put in a bucket in the root cellar. The amaryllises also get put into bags in the root cellar. I decide which beds will contain the carrots next year as it is best to prepare it with manure in the fall. The whole garden gets limed.

October

This is the month that I make sauerkraut and kimchee. The root cellar is nice and cold and any remaining cabbage that I covered during the frosts are brought in. I cover the spinach with clear plastic (on top of metal row covers) as soon as snow threatens. Spinach doesn't mind getting frosted; just don't pick it when it's below 32°F (it turns to mush). Wait until it warms up and turns

> Spinach doesn't mind getting frosted; just don't pick it when it's below 32°F (it turns to mush). Wait until it warms up and turns back into its lovely self.

37

back into its lovely self. October is also a good time to gather a couple of bags of kindling for the fall fires. Around the middle of the month is garlic planting time. Once the garlic is planted, I feel ready for winter. Mache for the winter salads is sown at this time.

November

I like to finish my holiday shopping before Thanksgiving so I spend some time doing this at the beginning of the month. I continue to pick spinach well into November and sometimes into December too. I take amaryllis out of the root cellar, one at a time about every two weeks. This gives us beautiful flowers for much of the winter.

I love Thanksgiving itself as it is such a celebration of the garden. We purchase a local bird and serve it up with our own veggies. Heavenly! A meal I can truly be thankful for.

December

The seed catalogues arrive en masse. They are full of beautiful pictures of midsummer bounty and they make my mouth water in anticipation. One year has been put to bed and another one is right around the corner. Life, truly, does go on.

Chapter Five

Planting the Veggies

Choosing the right spot in which to put your garden is key. It should be in a place that receives at least six (preferably eight) hours of Sun a day. It also shouldn't be close to tree roots which will steal water and nutrients, next to a road or driveway where vehicles can splash water from puddles onto it or in a low spot that stays wet after a rain. Check, too, that it isn't downhill from lawns or shrubs that receive lots of chemicals. It's also nice to have a pure water source nearby.

Once you have located the best space for your garden, it's time to get the soil ready. Good garden soil contains lots of humus (that water-retaining, dark earth that comes out of compost or aged manure). The area should be free of roots and rocks and easy to dig into.

Worms are a gardener's best friend so you want to create an environment that they would love. Adding soil amendments like organic alfalfa meal and kelp meal provide food for these industrious helpers (and your plants) so it's best to add some to the beds every year (a coffee can of alfalfa meal and a half coffee can of kelp meal will be enough for a bed three feet wide and eighteen feet long). Spread it around the top of the soil. A good way to ensure that there are some minerals in your beds is to add some Azomite® powder. The title stands for "A to Z of minerals including trace elements." Three quarters of a cup of this powder is good. After spreading these amendments, use a broad fork or a pitchfork to loosen up the soil all around the bed. You want the roots to be able to reach down into the Earth effortlessly. Testing the soil periodically will let you know what you need to add to keep the minerals in a proper balance.

If you are creating beds from scratch, you may need to add a bag or two of aged manure or compost. Local nurseries generally sell bags of these created from local sources. It's always best to go with sources that already come from your neighborhood. Big box stores often import them from other areas and you run the risk of introducing new pests or diseases into your garden if you purchase bags there.

Once everything has been added to the soil, rake it flat. You will know right away if you have enough good humus if it passes the water test. As you water, it will disappear into the soil. If it ponds and puddles on the top, you need more compost or aged manure.

Once the soil has been prepared, it's time to plant the crops. Each vegetable has its own likes and dislikes so use the guides that follow for tips on planting some of the most popular choices. The weather varies from year to year and creates differences in the yields. In a hot summer, the heat-loving plants will do best whereas in a cool one, the cold-tolerant ones thrive. Plant your favorites and keep your fingers crossed.

When weeding the garden, it's important to pull up all of the root since some weeds come back even stronger after they lose their tops. The best way to accomplish this is to loosen the soil around the weed with a gardening fork, then grab the weed slightly under the soil surface. Be sure to water the bed immediately after weeding to resettle the roots of the crop.

Lettuce

Lettuce is my husband's favorite garden item. Therefore, I plant it every ten to fourteen days all summer long. It has a tendency to get bitter as it ages so we like to eat the leaves when they are young (sweet and tasty!). I generally get the soil ready in an entire bed but only plant a few feet at a time. I broadcast the seeds (spread them all around instead of planting in rows). Then, I cover them with some compost or well-rotted manure. I often place a shell or some stones in the soil to mark how far the bed has been planted. The seeds get watered immediately.

I generally get the soil ready in an entire bed but only plant a few feet at a time.

Lettuce is fairly easy to grow. It needs to be consistently watered and thinned as the plants get bigger. I tend to sow seeds quite close together and bring all of the early thinnings to the chickens. Once they attain the size of a large spoon, I bring them in for salads and sandwiches. Lettuce grows low to the ground so it tends to be quite dirty. It's one of the crops that needs to be washed carefully. A salad spinner does a nice job drying off the leaves.

Kale

Kale is a wonderful and nutritious vegetable. It provides calcium, iron and carotenoids in abundance. It should always be eaten cooked in order to neutralize the oxalic acid that makes it harder to digest these elements. It is a really sturdy plant that can take several hard freezes and return to its lovely self. Kale is a must in my garden each year.

To plant, prepare the ground as usual. Kale is a bit of a heavy feeder so you might want to add some additional compost or aged manure. This plant can be sown before the frosts are finished; it is generally one of the first things that I plant. Make some dips or water catches a foot apart, sow several seeds around the dip and cover with 1/4 inch of compost or aged manure. I also leave some room at the edges of the bed to plant marigolds there later. Water well.

As the seedlings grow, I thin to one per dip. When harvesting, take the lower leaves first and the plants will continue to put out new leaves higher on the stem. My favorite way to eat kale is as a chip.

Kale Chips

1. Cut the leaves into two-inch (or so) squares. (The ribs are quite tough and should be discarded or added to soup stock.)

2. Brush the squares with good quality lard or olive oil and dust with salt.

3. Spread on a cookie sheet and bake at 360°F until crispy (about four to seven minutes).

Swiss Chard

Swiss chard is a member of the beet family. However, it is a beet that is grown primarily for its leaves. It is cold tolerant as well as heat tolerant and deserves a place in everyone's garden. I prepare the soil as usual. These seeds, however, like beet seeds, are not really seeds at all but rather a small fruit. Sow them thickly with rows about a foot apart in order to have a good germination. Then cover the seeds with about 1/4 inch of old manure or compost. When the bed is planted, water well. Like most other sprouts, you need to keep an eye on the moisture until the seedlings appear.

The sprouts reside in that top 1/4 inch of soil so it needs to stay moist. Once they emerge, they will need to be thinned.

As you thin, keep in mind that each plant needs room to grow. I thin slowly but often. The small plants can be added to salads or juiced. Once the plants get to be about four or five inches apart, you don't need to thin anymore. For harvesting, just cut the plant an inch from the base. It will grow back.

> For harvesting, just cut the plant an inch from the base. It will grow back.

Here is my favorite way to serve Swiss chard: Wash it and tear it into small pieces. Steam these pieces turning a few times. Once wilted, serve tossed with butter and grated cheese. Yum!

Swiss chard is actually a biennial. This means that it has a two-year cycle. The first year, it concentrates on putting out leaves; the second it will go to seed. Because it is cold tolerant, I sometimes leave my Swiss chard in the ground through the winter. It will often reappear in the spring. This is nice for an early harvest, but get it out, eat the greens and discard the rest of the plant. Otherwise it will just bolt into seed heads and die.

Mache

Mache is a popular European green that is especially high in carotenoids, essential fatty acids and minerals. I like to grow it in window boxes in a sunny window during the winter. It particularly likes cold weather; it usually won't even germinate if the temperature gets above 70°F. So, I start it outdoors in late October, once the weather here has started to turn cold.

Begin with two window boxes that have proper drainage holes, and fill them mostly with potting soil. Then sow the small seeds fairly thickly across the top; I broadcast instead of planting in rows. Cover with about 1/4 inch more potting soil and water well. Then, leave these window boxes outside so that the cold weather will encourage the seeds to germinate.

Because I sow thickly, the emerging plants look like little bunny ears everywhere. Once a hard frost threatens, I bring them inside. I thin the plants and add them to my winter CSA lettuce (or store bought). The two bunny ears will turn to four, then eight, then sixteen so I keep thinning and using them in salads. It may not be the bulk of the salad, but it is nice to have something so fresh and nutritious during the off season.

By the end of winter, there will be just two plants left in the window boxes but their greens will cover the entire surface. I bring these outside, let the bees pollinate their flowers all summer and collect the seeds for next year in late summer or early fall (before the frost). I spread them on a plate or cookie sheet for a few days to dry and place in a tightly covered seed jar.

Tomatoes

Tomatoes are, perhaps, the most-liked garden food. Nothing quite beats the taste of a big, luscious, sweet, thick, red tomato. Whether you quarter and toss them with mozzarella and basil or you slice and sandwich them with bacon and lettuce, tomatoes are the best. They are not particularly difficult to grow although they do better if you know a few tricks. Even someone with a sunny balcony (or roof) can grow tomatoes in pots. It's well worth the effort.

> Even someone with a sunny balcony (or roof) can grow tomatoes in pots. It's well worth the effort.

I buy small tomato plants rather than start them from seed. Let the nurseries who know what they are doing get these plants started for you in the best of circumstances. My favorite tomato plant grower has ninety-five heirloom varieties from which to choose. Tomatoes are extremely cold sensitive so it is best to wait until the weather has warmed considerably before putting them in the ground. Where I live, that's not until after the last full Moon before Memorial Day.

Tomatoes love manure. I prepare the beds as usual, but generally add an additional batch of manure or compost. Transplanting is ideally done in the evening, so, in preparation, I get the beds ready during the day. After raking them flat, I dig holes at least six inches down. I put cutworm collars on all of

my tomato plants. This consists of a ring of aluminum placed around the stem so that it is one inch above the soil line and one inch below. When the Sun begins to fade, I take the plants and plop them into the ground. Sometimes it is necessary to remove them from their pots and other times it isn't. Ask your nursery which kind of pot they use. You can plant tomato plants as deep as they will go since they will develop additional roots along the stem. Once inserted into the hole, secure the dirt around the stem. You want to get it snug so that the roots can settle. I also dig a small moat around the plants to catch any rain or water that comes their way. I like to put down a layer of newspaper (only the black and white sections that use soy ink) on the ground around the plants. This helps keep the blight at bay. Water immediately.

I also dig a small moat around the plants to catch any rain or water that comes their way.

As the tomato plants grow, they need to be supported. There are many different kinds of supports available and most garden centers will have a generous

assortment. I like the ones you can get from Gardener's Supply Company, especially their tomato ladders. I place the supports in the ground as soon as I plant them (or the next morning). I train the vines to stay inside the supports and limit the number of suckers (or vines) to three. The suckers will come at the junction of the main vines and a leaf. They either get pinched off or cut with small scissors (see before and after photos above). Many, many suckers are removed from the plants. Do be careful that you are not removing the flowers, though. They look different so check carefully.

The vines will need to be tied to the supports. I use cotton strips because string is too small and can damage the plants. I find unbleached cotton material in the remnants bin of a local fabric store where they can usually be had for little money. Then, I spend time watching TV or listening to the radio while cutting them into inch-wide strips.

When you see flowers forming on the tomato plants, they can use some additional potassium. I generally give them a foliar spray every five days or so. This is a liquid that often comes in a concentrate to be added to water. Do this either early in the morning or late in the evening. The plants will absorb this spray when the dew is still on them. Once the Sun has risen high into the sky, the spray will just burn off.

The tomato plants nearly always grow taller than my supports, so I also have some seven-foot stakes that go into the ground as they outgrow their ladders. By the second week of August, any flowers on the plants will never become ripe, red tomatoes so I cut them back. This encourages the plants to ripen the tomatoes that are left on the vines.

Most farmers pick their tomatoes before they are at the peak of ripeness. This is because—at the very peak of ripeness—a tomato is very easy to bruise. But if you leave it on the vine until it is a nice, deep red, the tomato will be utterly, indescribably delicious. It will also be nutritionally superior. If you don't grow your own, but get your tomatoes from a farmer, buy them a few days before you want to eat or process them. Put them on your kitchen counter and they will continue to ripen.

When I can no longer keep up with eating my bounty of tomatoes, it's time to put some of them in jars. Turn to the Summer In a Jar section in the Cooking chapter for directions.

Summer and Winter Squash

Whether you like yellow crookneck or green zucchini, summer squash is a true seasonal treat. Winter squash is an easy keeper and can be enjoyed quite a few months after the garden has been put to bed. Many nurseries sell plants that can help you to get a jump on the season. However, squash can easily be grown from seed right in the ground. They are terribly frost sensitive so they should definitely not be planted before all threat of frost has passed.

Prepare the soil as usual but you might want to add a bit of extra manure or compost as these plants really love the stuff. After raking the soil flat, make a large (two feet wide) dip or water catch (it looks like the top of a volcano), then place ten or twelve (or more) seeds around the dip and cover them with

1/4 inch of old manure or compost. I put in many more seeds than I am going to need because ants will often steal some. Water immediately and keep the area moist until the seedlings appear.

When the seedlings come up, let them grow for a

week or so to see which ones look most vigorous. Thin according to size and placement; you should end up with only three or four plants. Make sure that you have a lot of room outside of the dip for the plants to grow into. As the flowers begin to appear, it's quite easy to tell the males from the females; the females have little squashes on them. Some folks like to take a few (but not all) of the male flowers to stuff and cook (see recipes that follow). The females should be left alone.

Pick the summer squash fruit when it is still relatively young. About six inches in length is ideal. They need to be picked so that the plant will continue to produce more fruit. Sometimes a zucchini hides under the leaves and gets quite big. These can be used for zucchini bread or muffins. I feed them to my chickens.

Winter squash should stay on the vine until fully ripe. Most pumpkins will turn a nice, deep orange. Butternut gets tan. Hubbard turns a nice blue. Delicata gains green and tan stripes. Acorn and buttercup grow dark green. Spaghetti gets yellow.

Pick winter squash carefully. Make sure they have a good stem—if they are cut or bruised or lose their stem, they will not keep. In order for squash to last

many months into the winter, they need to be sunned (spaghetti squash doesn't keep all that well, but the others do). I place them in a sunny spot for about two weeks, turning them every few days. If a light frost threatens, bring them in or cover them. Definitely bring them in if a hard frost threatens.

48

Once they've been sunned, they are ready to keep. I simply place them on the beams in my living room where I can keep an eye on them. I put newspaper under each because when they deteriorate, it sometimes happens fast. The root cellar is too damp for these beauties. They need a dry environment. All winter long, these squashes add terrific vitamins and minerals to the diet.

Stuffed Squash Blossoms from Chef Billy Boudreau

> Pick winter squash carefully. Make sure they have a good stem—if they are cut or bruised or lose their stem, they will not keep.

1. Sauté one finely chopped shallot (or a small onion or three cloves of garlic) in a little olive oil.

2. Mix one egg with 1/2 cup Vermont Butter and Cheese goat cheese.

3. Add 1/2 cup cooked spinach (fresh or frozen), squeeze out as much water as you can.

4. Add the onion/shallot mixture. Season with salt and pepper and a dash of Worcestershire.

5. Stuff 12 blossoms. Delicately twist to seal and secure with a toothpick.

6. Dip each blossom into a bowl of two whisked eggs then into two cups of panko or fresh bread crumbs (you can add 1/4 cup grated parmesan to the breadcrumbs).

7. Bake in a 400°F oven for ten minutes or until browned.

Chevre Stuffed Zucchini Flowers with Basil Aioli from Chef Wesley Babb

In a mixing bowl, add filling ingredients:

6 ounces chevre
2 medium-sized shallots, minced
6 sprigs of thyme, picked
pinch of salt and pepper
dash of extra virgin olive oil

For the stuffing and breading of the flowers:

2 eggs
1/4 cup all-purpose flour
1/2 cup panko

1. Gently open the flower. Remove the stamen from inside and rinse with cool water.

2. Insert one ounce of filling per flower and softly twist to secure the stuffing inside.

3. Dip the flower into flour until coated. Dunk in egg wash and roll in bread crumbs until evenly coated.

4. Allow the breaded flowers to sit in the fridge for twenty minutes or so.

5. Fry in a pan with coconut oil or deep fry them until just crisp. (If they cook too long the cheese will burst out.) It's important to use low heat and pay attention to detail. This will produce a delicate tangy finger treat!

For the Aioli:

3 egg yolks
1/2 cup olive oil
2 cloves garlic
4 sprigs basil
2 Tbsp. lemon juice

1. Place the yolks and lemon juice in a mixing bowl and stir aggressively for thirty seconds.

2. While still mixing, add the garlic and slowly start adding the oil – just a bit faster than a dripping faucet.

3. Once the oil is all whisked in the texture should be similar to mayonnaise.

4. Chop the basil thoroughly and stir into the aioli.

5. Serve the crispy fried zucchini blossoms with the basil aioli and enjoy!

Cucumbers

To me, cucumbers are a real treat. They are crunchy, tasty and a fantastic addition to a salad. I often slice them, salt them and devour them as an afternoon treat. And, they make the best pickles.

To plant cucumbers, prepare the soil as usual. After raking it flat, broadcast the seeds a couple of inches apart, in about the center eight inches of the bed, then push them under the soil. This is two or three times more seeds than will be able to become plants, but, like other big seeds, ants will often steal some of them so I plant way more than I need. Be sure that no seeds are left visible to these voracious thieves.

Because I had to work so hard for every inch of garden space, I want all of it to work hard for me so I grow things up supports when possible. I like to grow cucumbers up a

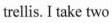
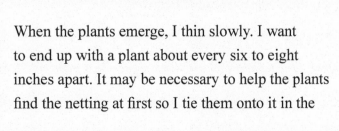

trellis. I take two garden posts and dig them in at the edges of the bed. I then place netting in between the posts and attach it securely with string.

When the plants emerge, I thin slowly. I want to end up with a plant about every six to eight inches apart. It may be necessary to help the plants find the netting at first so I tie them onto it in the

> # If a cucumber is left to mature, the plant will stop producing so look around carefully and take all the cukes that are ready.

beginning. After that, they will climb on their own. It's important to pick all cucumbers as they become ready (at about six to ten inches long depending upon the variety). If a cucumber is left to mature, the plant will stop producing so look around carefully and take all the cukes that are ready. Sometimes they like to hide under the leaves.

I not only make pickles with these veggies but I sometimes make cucumber "chips." I wash them and slice them thinly. Then I salt them and place them in my electric dehydrator. Once they are brittle (two to four days), they are ready to be put into jars in the pantry. These chips stay tasty all winter long.

Broccoli

Broccoli is a plant that can be put in the ground before all the frost is done. Garden centers sell the plants, but it is actually quite easy to grow from seed. I prepare my soil as usual. Then I create several dips or, as I call them, "water catchers" leaving about a foot and a half free at the ends of the bed and, if it is extremely long, also in the middle. These voids are where marigolds will be planted later to protect the broccoli from the cabbage moth.

The purpose of the water catchers is to catch rain and irrigation water and keep it right where the plants need it. I plant six or eight seeds around the inside edges of the dips and cover them lightly with compost or old, rotted manure. Then I water the bed well.

Once the broccoli plants emerge, I slowly (over the course of a couple of weeks) thin them, taking out the smallest ones first. As they continue to get bigger, the smaller ones get pulled until there is only one plant left in each dip.

After the danger of frost is gone, I plant marigolds in the spaces that were left free at the original sowing time. Two marigolds go into the ends and, if the bed is particularly long, two more in the middle. This helps tremendously to keep the cabbage moth away. The cabbage moth lays its eggs on all of the Brassicas. Out come little green worms that not only eat the broccoli but leave a mess behind them. With marigolds in place, remarkably few cabbage moths find the broccoli.

Broccoli is ready to pick when the head is full and firm. Be sure to cut the stem on an angle. Broccoli will continue to give you side shoots well into the fall, but water can sit in the stem causing it to rot it if it isn't cut on an angle. As the side shoots get smaller, I freeze them and write "quiche" on the bag. These are ready to go into eggs or stir-fries.

Freezing broccoli is very easy. It needs to be blanched (or steamed) for about three minutes, then placed in ice water to cool down and halt the cooking. After draining the pieces, I try to arrange them in freezer bags rather flatly so that they will stack easily. Early in

the season, when the buds are large, I just cut them into large serving-sized pieces before steaming quickly. These will go around the base of a baking chicken, on top of toast to be covered with a cream sauce or steamed as a side dish to be served with lots of butter and salt. As the season progresses and the shoots become small I freeze them in pints.

Bon appétit!

Peppers

Peppers are a real garden delight. Crisp, juicy and succulent they make terrific dippers and are a tasty addition to salads. Stir-fried, they soften and enhance the flavors of the onions and mushrooms or whatever else joins them in the pan. They are easy to preserve by freezing; I don't let a summer go by without putting some peppers away in the freezer.

A green pepper is really just an unripe pepper. As it ripens, it will turn red, orange, yellow, brown or purple. Many varieties are sweet while some others are hot. Paprika peppers can be planted if you'd like to make paprika powder at the end of the summer.

A green pepper is really just an unripe pepper. As it ripens, it will turn red, orange, yellow, brown or purple.

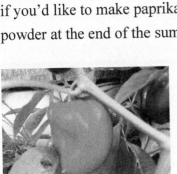

Pepper plants are especially sensitive to cold weather and will be harmed if set out too early in northern climates. It's better to wait an extra week or two to transplant these babies into the vegetable garden. They need lots of Sun and good, fertile soil. I plant my peppers about twelve inches apart and place eight or ten matches down in the hole with them. Each plant gets a cutworm collar (aluminum foil around the base of the plant that will cover one inch under the soil and one inch above the soil line). I cover the roots with the earth making sure that it is tamped down securely. Then, I water well.

Peppers like warm weather and take a long time to ripen. They don't have too many problems with insects but I keep an eye on them anyway. If frost threatens before the harvest is complete, they can be covered with sheets or towels or row cover (not plastic as the cold goes right through this substance). If a hard freeze is predicted, I will pull up the plants completely and wash the roots.

Then I hang them upside down on my porch where they will continue to ripen.

This is one of the easiest vegetables to freeze. I simply wash, dry and cut them into pieces (use rubber gloves if skin is sensitive) then place in a freezer bag, flattened so that they will stack nicely, and into the freezer they go. When I want to cook with them, they are easy to break off in small batches.

> It's a good idea to plant them twice as deep as the width of the seed, perhaps a bit more.

Pole Beans

Beans are extremely prolific in the garden. Even a small plot of them will produce many, many servings. After preparing the soil, I like to plant my pole bean seeds in a crater (like the top of a volcano). This provides a water-catch for them so that they can take full advantage of any rain or watering. Ants will often steal these seeds so I plant many more than I actually want to grow. I

place them all around the crater then push them under the top of the soil. It's a good idea to plant them twice as deep as the width of the seed, perhaps a bit more. I water them immediately.

Next, I construct a teepee out of bamboo poles. These plants need supports on which to grow and teepees work splendidly. I dig in six or eight poles around the circumference of the crater and tie them together at the top with some good sturdy twine. I may need to get the vines started growing up the poles but, once I do, the beans will continue to climb on their own.

After several weeks, flowers appear on the vines followed by teensy-weensy beans which quite quickly turn into bigger and bigger beans. It's important to pick them before they get too big as they become tough when very large. They love to hide in their foliage so it's necessary to lift up leaves and look under them. They grow fast, so it's good to check them every day or two.

Once I have satisfied my fresh bean craving, the rest go into the freezer. I sit with two bowls on my lap and a basket with the beans on a nearby table. One bowl is for the beans and the other is for the tops and bottoms. As I snap off the ends, I often also break the beans into two or three pieces. Shortening the pieces will make them easier to put in the freezer bags. The ends will go to the chickens or the compost. Next, I get some water boiling in my steamer and put some ice in an insulated container. Once the water has boiled, I put a handful of beans into the steamer and set my timer for three minutes. I fill a bowl with water and toss in some of the ice cubes. Using tongs, I toss the beans a few times while they are

Using tongs, I will toss the beans a few times while they are steaming.

steaming. Otherwise, the places where the beans lie upon one another will not get blanched.

When the timer buzzes, I put the beans into ice water to cool them down. After a few minutes, I place the beans in a salad spinner to remove the excess water. The beans are then sealed in a freezer bag and placed in

the freezer. I try to make the packages somewhat flat so they will stack nicely. I also often take a straw and, placing it inside one edge of the bag, I close up the top, suck out the extra air and finish the closure.

Asparagus

Asparagus is a perennial. It emerges every spring to a joyous welcome (nothing else in the garden is much available yet). The tender shoots have a unique and distinguished flavor. Steamed or stir-fried it can be a dish all on its own (with butter, naturally) or used in soups, stews or on beds of toast topped with cream or cheese sauce. Some also like it cold and marinated.

Once established, asparagus returns year after year with just a little attention and fanfare. Weeds, of course, need to be plucked away from it every summer and a watch must be placed on the asparagus beetle. In my part of the country, this beetle comes twice—once at the beginning of the season (late spring) and once again in the summer. These little bugs are sneaky, too; when they see me coming, they run to the back of the stem to hide. I knock them off the plant and into a container of water. The beetles are then thrown out onto the ground in the chicken run (chickens love beetles). If you don't have chickens, soapy water will also kill them. It's best to track them down early in the morning or late in the evening when it's cool.

As easy as asparagus is to keep, it is a bit more troublesome to plant. Most gardeners buy year-old "crowns" that resemble spiders with many legs (roots). These need to be planted at least a foot down, spread out for maximum surfacing and covered with loose soil (compost or old manure is best). Keep these tender plants well watered for the first year or two. Once the bed is mature, they will shade their soil handily as their roots go down quite far.

In the beginning, a few small stems appear. Do NOT cut them! This plant needs lots of time to establish itself and it takes a full two years. It's not until the third year that you can harvest asparagus. When the spears are about eight inches tall, cut or snap them. Pick any that are significantly thicker than a pencil and leave the rest. Don't touch the foliage in the fall until it is totally dead and brown, then it's best to burn it or haul it away to the dump as it may harbor asparagus beetle eggs. Fertilize regularly in the spring and/or fall and these wonderful vegetables will bring you much food and joy.

Potatoes

I have never met a potato that I didn't like. Fried, chipped, baked or mashed, potatoes are the ultimate comfort food. This is one vegetable that you should grow yourself or buy organic as it does have many insect pests and large, conventional growers often spray with toxic insecticides. I generally plant two different kinds of potatoes. My own personal favorites are Kennebec (for baking) and Caribe (for mashing). I always order my seed potatoes from an organic source. Home-grown potatoes are delectable beyond belief.

It is said that the ground is ready for potatoes when you see dandelions growing in fields. Two weeks before I want to plant them, I "green" them. To do this, I place the potatoes in a tray in a northern window. They should be in bright light, but not directly in the Sun. The light will cause them to sprout some tight, little sprouts.

Some people cut their potatoes, but I like to plant mine whole. I believe it is harder for disease to get started if your potatoes go in whole.

When you plant the entire potato, there is an obvious "up" and "down." The down is where the potato

attached to its plant when it was growing. There is a bit of an indent here and sometimes a little bump. On the opposite side is where most of the eyes (or sprouts) are. I always plant my potatoes with the sprout side up.

Prepare the beds as usual. Dig two furrows about a foot apart, piling the soil up around the furrows. Then dig down with a gardening spoon as far as it will go and insert the seed potato. You want the potatoes to be planted as deeply as possible because the new potatoes will grow above where you planted the seed ones. Cover the seed potato with soil and repeat about two feet down the furrow. When the entire bed is planted, water it well.

If frost threatens the plants after they come up, I simply cover them with the soil that is piled up on the side.

Potatoes are sensitive to frost but I plant them early anyway. They like to go into a cold soil and it takes a few weeks for them to emerge. If frost threatens the plants after they come up, I simply cover them with the soil that is piled up on the side. This keeps them safe. All of this soil will eventually be shifted next to the potato plant—as the plant grows, hoe the soil next to the stems. This is called hilling. Eventually, there will be hills where the furrows began.

The main threat to potatoes is the Colorado potato beetle. This insect usually shows up in early summer. Adults are almost fingernail-sized with a black and tan striped body and an orange-colored head. They lay light orange eggs on the bottoms of the leaves which turn into soft-bodied grubs. They can destroy the entire crop. I peruse my plants on a regular basis—in the early morning and evenings—and knock them into a container of water. These I throw into the chicken run and the girls eat them up. If you don't have chickens, put a little soap in the water to kill them.

The potatoes will grow and flower then appear to die back. Do not be discouraged; this is normal. I tend to leave my potatoes alone during the late summer months as there is so much else to eat at that time and potatoes are great keepers. When the root cellar has cooled down, it's time to dig the potatoes. Digging up the potatoes in the fall is—by far—my number one, most favorite thing to do in the garden. It's like finding buried treasure.

Start with a pitchfork at the outer edges of the bed. Be very careful not to spear the potatoes with the pitchfork, you just want to loosen the soil so that

> Digging up the potatoes in the fall is—by far—my number one, most favorite thing to do in the garden. It's like finding buried treasure.

you can get in there with your garden-gloved hands. The potatoes will be in the hills where you built up the soil around the plants. Carefully dig with your hands feeling around for the spuds. As you come across them, lift them out of the ground and place them on top. Sometimes you can use a small garden fork if the potato is wedged in. Once you have gone through the entire bed, go back over it with the pitchfork, turning the soil over completely. There are usually more potatoes to find.

Potatoes that are damaged in any way (speared, dinged or partially eaten) get set aside to be used first. The rest are left in the Sun for about twenty minutes, then turned over and left for another twenty minutes. Do not leave them in the Sun too long as they will turn green and become inedible (some potatoes have a green edge where the Sun did affect them—these are fine to keep, just cut off any green edges before you eat them or they could make you ill).

Potatoes are just about the easiest thing to store in the root cellar. They need to be fairly dry, then, using a small brush, gently clean each one and place it in a milk crate. Just don't try to stack the potatoes in the crates too high. The weight of the ones on top will mush the ones on the bottom and then you will have a big mess on your hands. Milk crates, however, can be stacked one upon the other.

The potatoes will keep in the root cellar all winter long. Come April, though, they know that it's time to be planted and will start to sprout. If you live in a colder climate (where winter lasts for months), then you can save your largest and best-looking potatoes to replant. However, if you live in a warmer region, do not bother to save any as there is too much danger of transmitting disease into your new plants.

Sweet Potatoes

Sweet potatoes are not only delicious, they are particularly nutritious and good for you. They are really a southern plant so, if you want to grow them in the northern states, you need to give them some extra care. Sweet potatoes are actually still alive even after they have been picked. They like to live in a warm environment such as on a counter or in a kitchen cupboard and they never should be placed in the refrigerator. Once they reside in an atmosphere that is below 50°F, they begin to die inside.

I wait until the weather has truly warmed before planting the slips that I mail ordered. The slips look fairly beat up when they first arrive, but they are still alive. I prepare the bed as usual. With my dibble (or pointed stick) I create a hole in which to place the roots of the slip. Firming the soil around the roots, I water immediately. The plants should be placed fairly far apart (two to three feet) as each is a vine which will spread out on the ground. Once the whole bed is planted, I take a sheet of clear plastic (not black) and place it over the entire bed. I cut holes where the plants are, use rocks to hold the plastic down and then bury the edges. It's important to have the plastic sitting right on the soil. Sweet potatoes like temperatures around 100°F (something that almost never happens in New Hampshire). The clear plastic helps to warm the soil.

> They like to live in a warm environment such as on a counter or in a kitchen cupboard and they never should be placed in the refrigerator.

As the vines grow, you can move them around a little in order to keep them out of the paths. Or, you can tie them up on a fence or support. They produce a lovely flower and make an interesting looking plant. Let them grow all summer long and into the fall.

Once frost threatens, the sweet potatoes need to come out of the ground and

get cured. I use a pitchfork to loosen the soil and dig them with my gloved hands. I place the pitchfork away from the plants and lift gently toward them. Sweet potatoes often corkscrew into the ground so they can be hard to dig up. Try not to cut them, but, if you do, they will survive. What they don't like is to be dropped or thrown. Handle them gently.

Once all the sweet potatoes have been harvested, I wash them. Then, they need to be cured in a room where the temperature can be maintained between 85°F and 90°F day and night for five days. A small room with a heater works best. I spread them out on a desk and check them daily. The sweet potatoes will actually grow a second skin during this process. Even the spots where the potatoes were cut will harden with a new skin. This skin will darken and feel almost tough.

> **Sweet potatoes taste better after they have been stored.**

After curing, I place the sweet potatoes in baskets around the house away from direct sunlight. They like to be warm, but not hot. If you choose a spot that's too hot, they will begin to sprout. Move them away from the heat source if this occurs. Sweet potatoes taste better after they have been stored. Some say not to judge their flavor until after New Year's.

Onions

I love onions. All my stir-fries start with one and all my meat dishes contain them (onions bring out the flavor of meat). If you want to have a steady supply of onions from your garden all year, start with varities that are known for their "keeping" qualities such as copra. These onions are usually quite strong and will make your eyes water when being cut.

I start my onions indoors in February. I fill two flats two-thirds full with potting soil. Then, I broadcast the onion seeds (sowing them everywhere and not just in rows) all over the top and cover with 1/4 inch more of potting soil. I water immediately. These flats are placed in a sunny southern window.

Onions germinate after a few days and put out a grass-like stem. They don't seem to mind being crowded so I never thin them. I keep an eye on the moisture and water when needed. When they get taller than four inches, I cut them back to the four-inch size. The onions that I plant are day-length sensitive. This means that they will send all of their energy into their tops while the days are getting longer and will begin to form a bulb (or root) when the days begin getting shorter. For this reason, I never give them extra light from a bulb at night.

> They don't seem to mind being crowded so I never thin them.

The onions continue to grow inside until it is time to put them into the garden. Onions can take a bit of frost so I generally plant them around the end of April. I prepare the bed as usual and rake it flat. Then I take my dibble (or a pointed stick) and create holes about four inches apart. Gently separating the onion plants, one goes into each hole. I tamp down the earth around the plant and move on to the next one. Once I have completed a bed, I water it well. I usually plant two full beds of onions as we eat them almost every day.

Onion plants are sensitive to drying out so I keep an eye on their need for water. I use a gardening fork to check the soil. Sending the fork down into the earth, it is definitely time to water if it comes up dry. The greens will grow and grow until, lo

and behold, after the solstice, they start to form bulbs.

By the middle of July, I let the onions dry out slightly more than I did in the spring and early summer. The second week of August is when I harvest them. Their tops should be falling over by this time. I pull them up and gently set them on a sheet in the Sun to begin the curing process.

You don't want the onions to get wet either with dew or rain because you are trying to harden the skins for storage.

At the end of the day, I carefully put them into baskets and bring them inside the house. You don't want the onions to get wet either with dew or rain because you are trying to harden the skins for storage.

The next sunny day, the onions go back out to cure and come back in at night. I do this for seven sunny days (it can take a couple of weeks to perform this task). Each day, I gently pull on the onion tops to separate them from the bulbs both when I set them out and take them in (wearing gardening gloves). By the last day, there usually isn't any green left on any of the onions.

Once the curing process is complete, they are ready to store in string bags for the winter. Any onions that are

damaged or have an opening at their top end go into a basket to use up right away. The rest are sorted into groups of small, medium or large onions and put into corresponding string bags. These bags hang in my pantry all winter long. Occasionally, an onion will start to sprout (and should be eaten right away), but if you have cured them properly and planted a "keeper" type, they generally last into June and July.

Garlic

Garlic never stops growing. From the minute it's put into the ground until the cloves plump up and are ready for harvest—and beyond—garlic continues to

grow. For this reason, the time to plant and harvest this particular plant is very regional. Those of us who live in the north plant garlic in the fall. It is planted in the winter elsewhere.

I generally save some of my garlic at harvest time to plant later on. Garlic cloves can also be bought from most local nurseries and catalogues.

Prepare the bed as usual. Separate the cloves and, using a dibble (a tool specific to planting garlic and onions) or pointed stick, poke holes about six inches apart and four inches down in the bed. Garlic does not like to be planted upside down so check the cloves to make sure you are planting them with the pointed side up. Place one clove in each hole. Cover

Garlic does not like to be planted upside down so check the cloves to make sure you are planting them with the pointed side up.

with soil. Continue with another row; I sometimes will stagger their placement so that the new row has garlic in between where the plants were in the previous one.

Water immediately. This shows the Devas and other overlighting beings (the spiritual entities that guide the crops through their various stages) that you are prepared to take care of the plants as they grow. Because our winters are long here in the northeast, I cover my garlic with the abundant leaves that have fallen from our many hardwood trees. I also generally hold the leaves down with the sunflower stalks from last summer's garden. The garlic will often grow a bit before the snow falls then continue to grow underneath after it snows.

In the spring, remove the leaves and other mulch. You will see the garlic poking up from under the ground. Water them when the soil is dry. Once the plants are well established, they will put up "scapes." This is like a flower on a stalk. You will want to remove them so that the energy of the plant will return to the bulb in the ground. The scapes can be eaten—try a nice stir-fry with chicken or beef.

When there are four green leaves left, it is time to harvest.

As the summer progresses, watch the number of leaves on the stalks. They begin with quite a few, then they turn brown and dry out. When there are four green leaves left, it is time to harvest. Here in the northeast, this generally occurs in mid-July. You want to be sure to pull them in time because, as I said before, garlic never stops growing. If you leave them in the ground after this point, they will lose their protective sheaths and start sprouting again.

Once the garlic is pulled, tie with string in bundles of eight. The bundles need to be hung in a breezy, shady place like a porch or open barn for at least two weeks to dry out. After this time, go through them and put aside the biggest ones to plant for next year. These I place in baskets in the pantry. Other loose garlic for eating can also be placed in baskets in the pantry—the hardneck varieties last quite a while. However, I like to dry them and make garlic powder which lasts all year long.

To make garlic powder, I begin by separating the cloves. Then, I slice a bit off of the top and the bottom of each clove (pulling to see if I can get anything extra off in the process). These go into the electric dehydrator at a temperature below 115°F. The low temperature helps to maintain the healing properties of the garlic. After one night in the dehydrator, I finish peeling the garlic and slice them up in my food processor. I put them back into the dehydrator for a good six or seven days, stirring occasionally. By this time, they are really dry.

I often leave a few of these small chips to put in my beet kvass (recipe on page 102) or to make into powder later.

However, most of these chips go into the blender and I hit the chop option.

Then, the resulting powder is run through a strainer to eliminate any large pieces which just go back into the blender. All of it eventually goes into clean glass jars, much of which is enjoyed in my cooking all year long and some of which is made into delightful gifts.

Beets

Beets are one of the most nutritious vegetables that we can grow in the garden. This dense, dark root is loaded with minerals and its flavor is distinct and strong. For this reason, nobody is neutral about beets. Folks either love them or hate them.

> On warm, sunny, windy days I may have to water these beds more than once.

The beet "seed" is not really a seed at all, but a small fruit. Each one will germinate several beets so thinning is essential right from the beginning. I prepare my beds as usual (I always plant several beds of beets) and I place the seeds in staggered rows about six inches apart. Beets should be planted fairly close together in order to get a good germination. Cover them up with 1/4 inch of old compost or manure and water immediately. As with most crops, I have to pay close attention to the moisture in the beginning. The sprouts will be living in the top 1/4 inch of soil until they get a chance to put down roots and push up leaves. On warm, sunny, windy days I may have to water these beds more than once.

As the beet leaves emerge, I check on them every few days. Each plant needs room to grow so I thin, thin, thin. I do this slowly, though, in case insects

damage some of the plants (or eat them). Thinning slowly betters my chances of having a nice harvest of large beets. When thinning, it is important to always take the smaller plant out first. It's quite tempting when the larger plant is getting to be an edible size to grab a few of these, but the larger seedlings will always give you a larger beet than the smaller ones.

Once the plants are a few inches tall, they can handle a bit of dryness on top of the soil. I don't want them to completely dry out, though, so I regularly check the soil by sending a gardening fork down into the bed. If it comes back completely dry, it's time to water. The best time to water is early in the morning or late in the evening. However, if things are very dry and it's almost noon on a hot day, I get them water right away.

The chickens or the compost pile get the thinnings until they are actually bite-sized. These early, small beets are incredibly tender and sweet. Don't forget to eat the greens as well (the greens actually contain even more vitamins and minerals than the beets). I wash them, tear them into small pieces, steam them (stirring occasionally) and toss them with butter and grated cheese before serving. To die for!

In the fall, the beets go into the root cellar. The timing is a bit tricky because the root cellar should be cool but there should not have been a frost yet. The larger the beet, the better it keeps so I begin by pulling up all the largest ones. By this time, the beets are growing up out of the ground so it is easy to see which are the biggest. Any that are nicked, dinged or partially eaten get put aside to use first. With the rest, I leave about an inch of leaves on the top and cut off the rest. It's important that the beets are fairly dry before they are

stored so I set them in the Sun for about twenty minutes or so, turn the beets over, and then leave them for another twenty minutes or so. Be careful not to leave the beets in the Sun too long or they might become inedible—if they turn green they can make you sick. Then I dust them off gently with a small brush and get ready to put them in their buckets.

I take a clean, dry, five-gallon bucket and place a layer of fine, dry sand on the bottom (use new material each year which can be purchased from a sand and gravel pit or garden centers). I then place the beets on top of this making sure that they do not touch one another. The whole lot gets covered by more sand; I generally start pouring it in between the closest beets so that they don't get forced together by this new sand. Once covered, I put in another layer of beets and cover them. I continue until the bucket is full. The cover then goes on the bucket and it goes into the root cellar.

I keep pulling the beets—again, largest first—until they are all in the root cellar. It's okay for the buckets to be stacked upon one another. When done, I know that I will have beets for stews and my favorite beet kvass well into the following July.

Carrots

Carrots are a wonderful vegetable to include in the garden plan as they are not only easy to store in the root cellar but they keep for many, many months. This delectable root is also used in many ways—steamed, juiced, grated, sliced for dips and added to stock broth. As delightful as carrots are, though, they are not the easiest vegetable to grow. Everything must happen just right for this plant to be happy.

To plant carrots, prepare the soil as suggested in the Planting the Veggies chapter. It's best to have manured the carrot bed in the fall in order to avoid the roots turning into multiples (forking). This vegetable is one that can be planted before the threat of frost has passed; however, depending on where you live, waiting a little longer may be worthwhile. I used to have a problem with the carrot maggot. At harvest time, many of my beautiful carrots would have these little worms eating into the tops near the greens thereby ruining them for storage. It was quite frustrating. Then, one day, I went on a garden tour and the leader explained that—in our area—the carrot maggot lays its eggs on May 21. If you plant your carrots before that date, the maggots will find them. Or, you can cover them with a row cover (fine material that lets in Sun and water, but not bugs) which prevents the maggots from laying their eggs. One year, I dutifully waited until May 22 to plant my carrots; however, it had been an unusually cold spring. Immediately, as soon as those little seeds were in the ground, flying insects began materializing everywhere and landing JUST on that bed. Luckily, I had some row cover. I smashed the bugs that had already landed and covered the bed right away.

Before planting, I take a couple of half buckets of soil out of the beds. Then, I plant my carrots in rows about six inches apart. I sow them fairly thickly as the germination rate isn't always what the seed packages claim and in case cutworms get some of them. Next, I take the scooped-out soil and cover the seeds with about 1/4 inch. Then, and this is critical, I water, water, water. Carrots take ten to fourteen days to germinate and

> Carrots take ten to fourteen days to germinate and they are notorious for dying off if they dry out even once during that time.

they are notorious for dying off if they dry out even once during that time. Remember, too, that these seeds are living in the top 1/4 inch of soil. This top layer is what needs to stay moist. On hot, sunny, windy days, I have had instances where I watered my carrots four or five times a day. If I have a need

It's so tempting to take the big ones when the little ones aren't amounting to much. Yet, the bigger ones will ultimately produce much larger carrots than the smaller ones ever will.

to be away for any length of time, I will sometimes cover the bed with wet burlap.

Once the tiny carrots appear, they are much easier to deal with. They need to be ruthlessly thinned so that the remaining plants have room to grow. In the beginning, the tiny seedlings can go to the chickens or the compost pile. Once they attain the size of a small finger, they go into the dinner pot. It is important, however, to always thin out the smaller carrots. It's so tempting to take the big ones when the little ones aren't amounting to much. Yet, the bigger ones will ultimately produce much larger carrots than the smaller ones ever will. The tops of the carrots are also edible. They can be added to stocks or made into juice.

As fall approaches, it's time to get the carrots into the root cellar. The timing here is a bit tricky; you want the root cellar to be cool but you also want to get the carrots into it before a frost. A frost can damage the roots making them unstorable. The bigger the carrot, the better it keeps so I begin by pulling up the biggest carrots. Any that are dinged, chipped, forked or eaten get put aside to be used

quickly. With the rest, I cut off most of the top leaving about an inch. I leave the carrots in the Sun for about twenty minutes or so. I then turn them over and leave them in the Sun for another twenty minutes or so. You want the carrots to be dry, but don't leave them in the Sun too long or they will become inedible. They will turn green and can make you sick.

Taking a clean, dry five-gallon bucket, I place a small layer of clean, fine sand on the bottom. Brushing the carrots with a small brush, I place them on top of this sand but not touching one another. The carrots then get covered with sand. I usually start this process by putting sand in between the carrots that are the closest together. This prevents the rushing sand from forcing the carrots together. I do the same with the next row and the next one until the bucket is full. The cover goes on and it goes into the root cellar. When I take out a carrot next winter, spring or summer, it's just like it came right out of the garden. I can juice it, steam it, stew it or grate it. It's wonderful.

When I take out a carrot next winter, spring or summer, it's just like it came right out of the garden.

Cabbage is a member of the Brassica family (like broccoli, Brussels sprouts, cauliflower and kale). It doesn't mind a bit of frost so it is one of the first beds that I plant each spring. It's easy to grow cabbage from seed—especially if you get it going in the ground early. Many nurseries also sell cabbage plants but unwanted bugs can come with them, so I always plant from seeds.

> ## Many nurseries also sell cabbage plants but unwanted bugs can come with them, so I always plant from seeds.

Prepare the bed as usual. Cabbage plants are heavy feeders so I sometimes

add a little extra old manure or compost. After the bed is raked smooth, I make circular pits (like the top of a volcano) with my gloved hands. These I call "water catchers." I also leave space at both ends of the bed and in the middle if the bed is large. Later on, I will plant marigolds in these spaces to help ward off the cabbage moth. I then place several cabbage seeds in each of the pits and cover them with 1/4 inch of old manure or compost. When the bed is planted, I water well. Remember to keep the topsoil moist until the plants emerge.

Once the plants come up, I let them grow for a while. I often have damage from cutworms, nasty little critters that come up at night and take one bite out of a plant—right where the plant goes into the soil (thereby killing the whole plant). They then burrow back down into the soil so you can't find them in the morning. If I find that they are bothering my cabbage, I will put cutworm collars on some of the plants. This is tin foil that I wrap around the base of the plant going about an inch into the soil and an inch above it. I then get some diatomaceous earth and sprinkle it around where the damage occurred. Diatomaceous earth is actually the fossilized skeletal remains of diatoms (aquatic organisms). It dries out and kills the insects that come into contact with it. It's best to use sparingly as it destroys all insects, including the beneficial ones.

Once the plants are well established (about five or six inches tall), I thin them to one or two per pit. I keep the bed weeded and uniformly moist. I don't generally harvest my cabbage until late in the fall. They can be pulled out of the ground with their roots intact. I then wash the roots and hang them upside down in the root cellar. They will keep for at least six weeks there.

I grow cabbage mostly for my own version of kimchee (a fermented food which gives me not only digestive enzymes, but probiotics too). See recipe on page 103.

Basil

Basil is a lovely, aromatic herb that is delicious in sauces, dips and pesto. It is extremely frost sensitive so should not be planted until all danger of frost has passed. I prepare the bed as usual then broadcast the seeds (send them everywhere, not just in rows). Then I cover with 1/4 inch of old manure or compost and water well.

As the basil plants emerge, I thin them so that the ones remaining have room to grow. Make sure that the leaves of the plants aren't touching the leaves of the one next door. I thin slowly, giving the first ones to the compost pile or the chickens and the later ones brought inside to use in recipes. As the plants begin to get big, I will cut off the tops. This makes them bush out more. I may

need to thin some more so that the remaining plants have enough room to grow.

Don't let them flower as this will change the flavor of the basil.

These plants will continue to grow all summer long. Don't let them flower as this will change the flavor of the basil. I like to dry some to use during the winter in dips. Pick, wash and spin the leaves. Then place on a cookie sheet in an oven with a pilot light on and the door closed or set the oven to the lowest temperature with the door slightly open. Or, set in an electric dehydrator. Once they are crispy and disintegrate when touched, I let them cool then store in tightly closed glass jars.

In the winter, I get some sour cream and crumble the basil into it along with some sun-dried tomatoes. It's best to make up this dip a day or two before you want to use it. Yum!

Chapter Six

Preserving Your Bounty

Many places in the world have seasonal gardens. This means that there are stretches of time (sometimes short and in some places, long) when the outdoor larder is empty or frozen. During these periods, you can be dependent upon the items of food that you have preserved in some form. The following sections will help you do just that!

Drying Tomatoes, Paprika and Herbs

Drying is one of the oldest forms of preservation in the world. Evidence shows that many indigenous tribes used the technique as a way to preserve foods for colder or drier times. There is also evidence of drying methods used by Roman, Middle Eastern and Oriental cultures dating back to 12,000 B.C. Some herbs can be spread out in the sunshine but most require a drafty shade to maintain their color and nutrients.

Bushy herbs that have leaves coming off stick-like branches (oregano, thyme, tarragon or mint, for example) can be picked, washed, spun dry and then tied in bunches to hang from the ceiling or out on a windy, protected porch. Or, they can be placed on a cookie sheet in the oven with a pilot light on or set to the lowest setting (the latter with the door slightly ajar). An electric dehydrator is another option. The herbs are truly dry when they crumble and should then be put into tight-sealing glass jars. Parsley and basil can also be dried in this manner.

Tomatoes and paprika, however, really need a bit more power than the oven method so I use an electric dehydrator. When choosing tomatoes, I like a paste variety as there is less water in

The thinner the slice the quicker they dry. However, I find that if I cut them too thin, they stick to the tray and become difficult to remove.

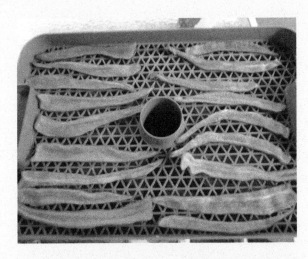

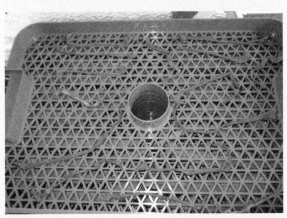

the flesh. San Marzanos are my favorite. I wash and dry the tomatoes, then cut them into slices. The thinner the slice the quicker they dry. However, I find that if I cut them too thin, they stick to the tray and become difficult to remove. Quarter-inch slices have worked best for me. I lay them flat on the tray and set the dehydrator to 125°F. After a few hours, I briefly raise them up with a spatula then put them back down so that they won't stick. The next day, I turn them over. At the end of a few days, they are nice and

81

dry and ready to use in recipes. I want them to be almost crispy so that I can grind them up and use them in dips.

Paprika is made from actual paprika peppers. I buy the young plants from some local nurseries and transplant them in beds like the other peppers. As the peppers mature, I cut them from the plants. Then, wearing rubber gloves, carefully wash, dry and slice them into ribbons, discarding the internal seeds (I give mine to the chickens). These ribbons go onto trays and are dried at about 125°F. It takes a few days for them to get brittle enough to be ground into powder.

This powder makes an excellent gift and is a great addition to quiches, deviled eggs and other egg dishes.

Freezing Berries

Berries are some of the most nutritious food items that we can grow or buy. Blueberries and blackberries are loaded with antioxidants and just about anybody can make a little room in the freezer to preserve some (this can also be done with elderberries, strawberries, cranberries, huckleberries, raspberries and boysenberries). There are many places where folks can pick their own berries to save some money. Berries that grow on tall bushes have the added advantage of being clean when picked so there is no need to wash them.

I collect berries using a yogurt container I hang from my neck with twine. This leaves both hands able to pick. I bring other containers with me to dump the berries into as they fill, so it doesn't ever get too heavy.

Freezing them on cookie sheets also allows them to freeze individually, rather than in a big glob.

With blueberries, I pick the bluest ones; those still purple will be a bit tart. With blackberries, the blackest are the best—a little red means that they are still a bit tough.

Once I have picked my fill, I transfer the berries onto cookie sheets. This way, I can look them over and eliminate any stems, twigs and leaves that found their way into the container. Freezing them on cookie sheets also allows them to freeze individually, rather than in a big glob. Once frozen, they can be transferred to freezer bags. If you just put them in the freezer bags initially, they will all mush together in one big ball.

These berries can then be used in smoothies, fruit kvass, with yogurt or ground up and added to flavor kombucha (a fermented drink loaded with probiotics). Yum!

Freezing Corn

Of all the things that I do in the summer, freezing corn, I think, is the biggest bang for the buck. It's the easiest yet most productive task for the time involved. I don't actually grow corn. Corn needs to be grown in a big stand; it's not pollinated by bees, but by the wind. Each piece of silk is connected to a kernel and each kernel needs to be pollinated to grow. So I buy my corn from a local, organic farm.

Of all the things that I do in the summer, freezing corn, I think, is the biggest bang for the buck.

Corn goes from a sugar to a starch quickly once it is picked so it's important to freeze it soon after it is harvested (preferably within six hours). I go to the farm stand first thing

in the morning and buy about two and half dozen ears. Once home, I get the water boiling to either steam it (more nutrition) or boil it. Then I go out and start shucking. Once the ears are all stacked on a tray, I bring them into the house and fill a small insulated container with ice. I get out my largest bowl and I'm ready to go.

Six ears at a time go into a large steamer for three minutes. I use a timer to keep track of the minutes. While they are cooking, I fill a large bowl with cold water and eight ice cubes. When the timer dings, the ears get plunged into the cold water. This stops the cooking process and gets them ready for the freezer. It generally takes a few minutes for the ears to cool and I leave them in the ice water until they do. Next, I place the ears on a table

in front of me. Putting one end of an ear at a time in a bowl, I use a sharp knife to cut the kernels from it. When the bowl starts to get too full, I take a spoon and fill some quart freezer bags already marked with the year. Three ears often fill a quart bag and I flatten it out so that it will stack nicely. I then take a straw and insert it into the top of the bag. Closing the bag on the straw, I suck out the extra air, whip out the straw and finish closing the bag. Then into the freezer it goes.

I usually get seven or eight quarts of corn from two and a half dozen ears. Even though the farm stand is a good

So for four hours of work and a small amount of money, I have beautiful sweet corn all year long.

fifteen minute drive from my house, it only takes me two hours from the time I leave to get the corn until it is in the freezer. I do this twice in the summer. So for four hours of work and a small amount of money, I have beautiful sweet corn all year long.

The Root Cellar

Our ancestors preserved their bounty differently than we do today. Without the benefit of electricity, they dried, they fermented and they stored root crops in their root cellars. Even if you don't have a garden, you can still take advantage of a root cellar. Beets, carrots, potatoes and turnips are ideal candidates. Farmers will often sell large quantities of these vegetables at a discounted price while they are in season. Ask that they not be washed for best results.

Don't have a root cellar? Well, if you have any kind of regular cellar that is unheated but doesn't freeze, it's quite easy to build one. All you have to do is create a room that is critter-proof.

A heated basement requires a bit more planning. Find the corner which is farthest away from a source of heat. Here you can build a small (or large) room utilizing insulation, a door and some shelves. The earth, itself, generally stays around 55°F so isolating the veggies in this particular corner will help to preserve them.

The vegetables in a root cellar need fresh sand each year so I generally bring several buckets, a shovel and a hard hat to a local gravel pit/materials business. The owner of my local facility actually gives me the sand for free so I always bring him some fresh veggies in exchange. Since the sand

Since the sand can't be re-used in the root cellar next year, I use it on the driveway and walking paths when they get slick in the winter.

can't be re-used in the root cellar next year, I use it on the driveway and walking paths when they get slick in the winter.

Root vegetables for storing must be in absolutely perfect condition; those with nicks, cracks and tears should be left in the kitchen to eat immediately. When it's time to harvest, I pull the veggies up out of the ground and let them dry out in the Sun for about twenty minutes on each side. They shouldn't be left in the Sun for too long or they will turn green and spoil. Once this type of vegetable is green, it is indigestible and can make you sick. I then cut the tops off, leaving about an inch of greenery, and wipe them gently with a brush. Using fresh, dry sand, I cover the bottom of a five-gallon bucket. Next, I place

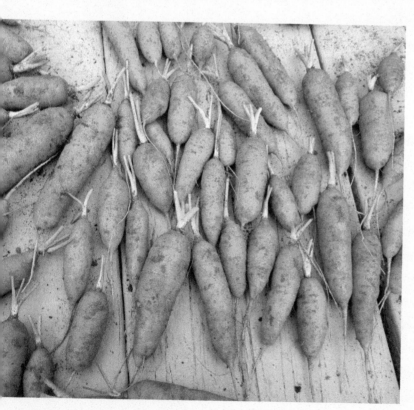

the vegetables on top of the sand, not touching each other. I cover the layer of vegetables with sand and add more veggies in the same way, working my way up the bucket until it is full, then top the bucket off with sand. Placing a lid on top, into the root cellar it goes. My storage space doesn't have any shelves so I stack the buckets on top

of each other and they do just fine.

Potatoes are the easiest to store of all. They only require a few minutes in the Sun (or shade) to dry, just long enough so the dirt is easy to brush off. Again brushing softly, I place them in milk crates. They don't need any other special treatment but be careful not to stack them too deeply. The weight of the ones on top can cause the ones on the bottom to bruise. Once bruised, they will rot from the bottom to the top.

Never put apples into the root cellar with your vegetables. They give off ethylene gas which causes other crops to ripen and go by more quickly. In fact, I often use apples to ripen my avocados. When I buy avocados, I always buy an apple and tuck them together in a paper bag for a day or two to finish ripening them. Works like a charm.

Never put apples into the root cellar with your vegetables. They give off ethylene gas which causes other crops to ripen and go by more quickly.

Chapter Seven

Cooking

Cooking from scratch is a fantastic way to express your creativity and save lots of money. Some people are intimidated by the thought but, if you use quality, fresh ingredients, you almost can't go wrong. I use cookbooks for ideas but long ago gave up running to the store to buy celery when there was broccoli available in the garden. So, I'm a theme chef instead of a recipe one.

Certainly, the most difficult aspect of cooking is to have everything on the plate done at the same time. Cookbooks are essential for the timing of different roasts (a meat thermometer also comes in handy here). However, other staples are fairly consistent in their baking times. Potatoes take about two hours at 350°F to become soft in the middle as do whole carrots, beets, onions and turnips that are added to the pot of roasting chickens or other meats. Cut up root vegetables can be steamed in about one hour. I often cook these and other veggies in soup stock then add the mix to a stir-fry thickened with arrowroot (similar to cornstarch but with the added benefit of useful minerals) and serve over pasta.

I often hear people complain that free-range meats are too expensive. And, it's true—I did pay a premium for my free-range Thanksgiving turkey. However, we had a feast on Thanksgiving, turkey pot pie the next day, hot turkey sandwiches the day after that and another repeat of the holiday meal two days later. I also put three large bags of turkey meat in the freezer (each one will provide us with several days of sandwiches) and made a humongous pot of stock from the bones which I cooked on the woodstove. For the same amount of money I spent on several days' worth of turkey dinners, I could have dined once at a local restaurant with two of my friends.

Being clever with leftovers is a great way to save money. For example, when we eat hot dogs, we never eat the whole package. There are always at least a couple left in the bag. So, I cut them up small and stir-fry them in coconut oil or butter then toss my scrambled eggs in the pan with them. Delicious! Or, there are some people in my family who are not fond of dark turkey or chicken meat in their sandwiches. So sometimes I put the meat through a meat grinder and jazz it up with homemade mayonnaise and Worcestershire sauce. Bite-sized meat and vegetable bits can be thrown into the freezer

> **For the same amount of money I spent on several days' worth of turkey dinners, I could have dined once at a local restaurant with two of my friends.**

for future stocks. Also, I always bake extra potatoes when my oven is going because later I love to cut them up and fry them in good quality lard or goose fat (exquisite!).

A couple of years ago, I made a quiche for a neighbor's party. When I went to pick up my pan, a woman said, "That's the best quiche I have ever tasted. What is your recipe?" I gave her my recipe but it wasn't until later that I realized that the true worth of the quiche came from the fresh ingredients: my own fresh eggs, onion, peppers, broccoli and spinach, and fresh raw milk right from a local farm.

Stir-fries can be made using almost anything. Mine always start with an onion and some red peppers cooked in coconut oil, butter or lard until the oil becomes red and the contents have softened. This takes about twenty minutes or more. Then I add cut-up steak, chicken, turkey or pork. Toss in some cooked carrots, frozen broccoli, corn or peas, heat them up and a feast awaits.

Marinades are a great solution to soften a tough steak or to spice up chicken and pork. Salad dressings often make wonderful marinades. I find it extremely difficult to find quality fats in most store-bought salad dressings, so I make my own homemade vinaigrette with organic olive oil and organic balsamic vinegar. Not only is it yummy but it is also good for you. The vinaigrette works as a great marinade for tough steak and I love to marinate chicken or pork in fresh garlic and tamari soy sauce.

Homemade Vinaigrette Dressing and Marinade

1. In a pint jar, fill about 1/5 with balsamic vinegar and about 3/5 with olive oil.

2. Add a few dashes of my homemade garlic powder (or a couple of diced or squeezed fresh cloves, if in season), about 1/4 teaspoon of powdered mustard, a few dashes of salt and a tablespoon of maple syrup.

3. Refrigerate.

When making a salad:

4. Get out a small glass measuring cup and stir up one raw egg yolk (Please only add a raw yolk if you can be sure that your eggs are disease-free otherwise see Step 6).

5. Add a few finely chopped anchovies.

6. A mashed strawberry or two (in season) can be added to the mix instead of the egg yolk and anchovies.

7. Then add three to five teaspoons of well-stirred olive oil mix (which I often leave on the counter for fifteen minutes ahead of time to soften).

8. Stir well and toss onto salad.

> **Believe it or not, you can wrap all the fillings for tacos in lettuce!**

Many folks are now interested in decreasing their consumption of grains. Tacos, sadly, are on that list. But there is a way to eat them without corn or wheat wraps. Believe it or not, you can wrap all the fillings for tacos in lettuce! Take some large lettuce leaves, wash and spin dry. Place the meat, cheese, avocado, crème fraiche, tabasco and whatever else you choose in the middle of the lettuce leaf. Roll up and devour!

Here is another recipe I will share with you for a sauce that I like to put on white fish (cod or halibut, for example).

White Fish Sauce

1. Melt 1/2 cup butter.

2. Wash, dry and cut a bunch of small, or two or three large, mushrooms (I like crimini or portabella) to any size that you would like and place in a shallow pan.

3. Mix melted butter with 1/2 cup Worcestershire sauce and pour over mushrooms.

4. Cook for one-half hour, turning the mix halfway through at around 350°F.

5. Pour over fish when serving.

Experiment! Don't let anything go to waste. Make salad croutons with bread that is starting to get old or create a soup with leftover butternut squash. Think. It needn't be complicated and all of these homemade meals

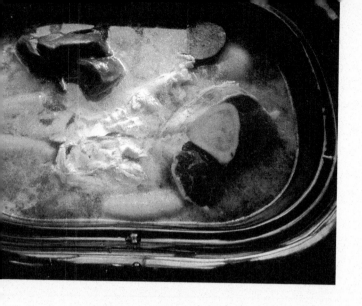

are so much better for you than anything that comes in a package.

Bone Broth Soup

Bone broth soup is magical. I made a startling discovery over twenty years ago (I don't even honestly remember how I made it), but—if my husband and I have at least two servings of my homemade bone broth soup a week—we have no problems with our joints. If we don't, my knees really bother me and Bob complains about feeling "creaky."

So how do I make my soup? I start with good quality bones (from verifiable cage-free animals that got to roam in the fresh air and sunshine); they can be chicken, turkey, beef or lamb. There should be some meat on the bones because that is where the flavor lies. Then, I always add a few chicken feet. The highest amount of gelatin in a chicken is in the feet. I also add some carrots, beets, onions, a small piece of good quality liver (from any pastured animal) and, in the summer, greens. Beet greens, carrot tops, Swiss chard, spinach and kale can all add valuable vitamins and minerals to the soup. Remember, most vitamins and minerals are water-soluble (they dissolve in water) so they go *into* the soup. A few tablespoons of white wine or vinegar also helps to bring the goodies out of the bones.

I cook this all together on low for two days. It's important to keep it at a low simmer—not a rolling boil. In the

> Remember, most vitamins and minerals are water-soluble (they dissolve in water) so they go *into* the soup.

winter, I cook it on the woodstove. In the summer, it goes into the crock pot. If you don't have a crock pot, you can start it on the stove and move it into the oven (200°F) after it comes to a boil.

This process transfers the vitamins and minerals into the liquid. After two days, I put it all through a colander and strainer and funnel the broth into "can or freeze" pints which then go into the freezer.

Local farmers often have soup bones for sale at a bargain price. Chicken feet can also usually be found at farm stores and farmers' markets. If you buy carrots at the farmers' market, ask for the tops to come with them. Bits and pieces of vegetables like cabbage cores and kale stems can be thrown into the freezer for a couple of weeks and saved for soup making. If you buy chicken at the supermarket, always get it with the bones. If they don't carry chicken with bones, request it. The price is always cheaper per pound so the bones are, in essence, free. Then save these bones in the freezer until you have enough to make a soup.

This soup can be heated and eaten as is. Or, for a heartier soup, you can sauté some onions and red peppers, add the soup and cook in more of your favorite veggies (carrots, beets or celery). Or, you can make it into gravy (heat until boiling then add some arrowroot mixed with cold water). Yum!

Canning Tomatoes

Tomatoes are right up at the top of folks' list of favorite summertime foods. There is nothing like a beautiful, bright red garden tomato for flavor and nutrition. Of course, this is a seasonal treat which absolutely cannot be replicated in the winter months.

The hard, plastic-like supermarket tomatoes found in other seasons (to me) don't even come close to resembling the real summertime treat.

The good news is that most tomatoes are naturally acidic and preserve beautifully by canning. However, there are some lower acid tomatoes such as Amana Orange

> The lycopene (a critical nutrient for corralling free radicals, prostate health and cancer prevention) actually increases when tomatoes are cooked.

and Orange Queen which are more susceptible to botulism so these (and other) varieties are not recommended for canning. Botulism occurs in an alkaline environment and is very dangerous (it can kill you). Supermarket cans containing botulism will bulge outwards. Never eat the contents of a can that sprays outwards when you open it. As I take off the screw bands, the lids would loosen if something of this nature occurred. So **never** eat the contents of a jar that has lost its seal.

Tomatoes don't like to be cold but love the heat and they don't seem to mind going through intense processing. The lycopene (a critical nutrient for corralling free radicals, prostate health and cancer prevention) actually increases when tomatoes are cooked. I like to can my tomatoes with a few other ingredients.

Summer in a Jar (Garden Delight)

I start with a bit of olive oil, some diced onions and red peppers (plus a dash of salt). Stirring often, I let these onions and peppers cook until the oil begins to look red (about twenty to thirty minutes). While they are sautéing, I wash the tomatoes and get a medium pot of water boiling on the stove. Once all

the tomatoes are clean, I dip them into the boiling water for about thirty seconds to loosen the skins. I can usually fit three to five tomatoes (depending on their size) at a time in the boiling water. You can actually see the skins beginning to come off of the fruit. Then they immediately go into a pan of cold water. The cold water will need to be replaced often. After several minutes, back onto the counter they go.

Once all of the skins have been loosened, I place a large bucket on old newspapers on the floor. The "traditional" way to proceed would be to take the skins off, throw them in the bucket, place the tomatoes on a cutting board and slice them into pieces (putting the core also in the bucket). I believe the way I do it is much more fun. Being sure that my hands are really clean, I stand over the bucket and slip off the skins. Then I hold the tomato over the pot with the onions and peppers and squeeze it into small pieces, which drop into the pot. The core goes into the bucket. It kind of reminds me of the old "I Love Lucy" show where she stomped on the grapes. It really is quite fun.

The pot will need nearly constant stirring at this point. The burner should be on a low setting but the bottom of the pot can easily burn if it is left alone. Now, the brew is ready for herbs.

I love garlic. This pungent bulb is not only delicious but filled with anti-bacterial, anti-viral and anti-fungal agents. A garlic bulb actually has two primary components in its cells (alliin and alliinaise) that are separated by a cell wall. It is the coming together of these two components once you chop or press the garlic that results in the formation of allicin—the medicinal element. So, when using garlic in recipes, it is wise to chop, mash or press the garlic

When using garlic in recipes, it is wise to chop, mash or press the garlic into a side dish and let it rest for about ten minutes before putting it in the recipe. This allows the allicin to form.

into a side dish and let it rest for about ten minutes before putting it in the recipe. This allows the allicin to form.

I also like to add fresh basil, thyme and oregano to the mix. I wash these thoroughly and set them on the counter. The basil leaves get broken into smaller pieces then go into the pot next (without the stems). Sometimes I break the oregano leaves if they are too big as well. Again, I discard the stems. Usually the thyme is small enough to go in as a whole leaf (no stems). Continue to stir frequently; the mix is now ready to can.

At this point, I get the canner steamer going. There are actually two types of canners: a water-bath and a steamer. I prefer the steamer as it uses less water and fuel. It's not as precise as the water-bath, though, so if you're skittish you might want to use one of those instead.

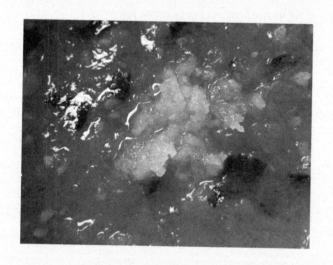

Make sure that the jars you will be using are clean. The lids also need to be washed as they come out of the box. New lids are essential every year (or time) as the rubber on the bottom of the rim gets exhausted by the canning process. Salt is an important ingredient in preservation so add 1/2 teaspoon to each pint and one full teaspoon to each quart. I put a jar topped with a stainless steel funnel next to the tomato pot. Carefully doling out the mixture with a stainless steel ladle, I fill the jar until it is almost full (pints need 1/2 inch head space—air at the top—and quarts need a full inch). Then I take a clean rag and very carefully wipe the rim of the filled jar. This is a VERY IMPORTANT step. If even a tiny speck of food remains on the rim, the jar will not seal properly. Placing the lid on the clean rim, I put a screw band around the top, screw it down and ease the jar into the canner. I continue this process until the canner is full.

If even a tiny speck of food remains on the rim, the jar will not seal properly.

The lid now goes on the canner. If you are using a water-bath canner, leave the heat on high until the whole lot of water covering the jars by an inch is boiling. If you are using a steamer canner, wait until there is a steady stream of six inches of steam coming out the two holes on the sides (be sure to place the holes where the steam won't burn you). Set the timer for thirty minutes for pints and forty minutes for quarts.

Once the timer dings, turn off the heat. Lift the lid carefully being sure that you send the steam away from you (to the back). Gently lift out the jars and place them on a cooling rack. Move them slowly as a fast journey could crack the jars. Also be sure not to put them in a draft as the same thing can happen. You will hear the lids start

Gently lift out the jars and place them on a cooling rack. Move them slowly as a fast journey could crack the jars.

to seal as they pop (a heavenly sound!). You will know that each jar has sealed when the little button in the middle of the lid gets sucked down.

After the jars have cooled, remove the screw bands. The jars will remain sealed without them now. Often, during processing, some food will leak out onto the bands. Washing them immediately keeps them fresh and rust-free for the next batch. I always mark the lids with the name of the mix and the year. The lids are going to be thrown away so this eliminates having to scrub the labels off the jars themselves. These treats are now good to store for up to two years. I always have a few jars left over from the previous year so I pull these to the front when I put the new jars away.

When deciding whether or not a jar is still edible, look for several things. First of all, the seal should remain unbroken (when opened, the jar makes that nice sucking sound). Also, the color should be just as bright as the day you canned it and the contents should smell terrific. If the seal is broken or it looks or smells bad, throw it out.

I use the mixture in these jars primarily in soups. Or, I will cook some elbow macaroni right in the mix and add it to some fried onion and hamburger for American chop suey. Yum!

> ...I use two pots when making sauce; the evaporation happens faster when using an additional pot.

Spaghetti Sauce

I start my spaghetti sauce the exact same way that I do the Garden Delight. However, add just a tiny bit of grated beet and carrot to the ingredients in the pot. I want to be careful to keep the mix acidic (to avoid any possibility of botulism) so I don't put in too many root vegetables. Adding a few makes the sauce nice and sweet. Skip this step, though, if it makes you nervous. Another difference is that I use two pots when making sauce; the evaporation happens

faster when using an additional pot. This mix really needs to be babysat with stirring, especially when it begins to thicken. It generally takes several hours for the sauce to condense. I have to scrape the sides of the pot often as the mix sticks to it and some sauce can be lost as the level goes down. Once the sauce looks like it might stand up on the plate, I often add a jar or two of commercial tomato paste (organic and sealed in glass jars). This makes it really thick.

The canning process for the sauce is exactly the same as for the tomato mix. I mostly use quarts and pints but sometimes will can a few smaller jars such as half pints as I love it on tacos or homemade pizza. This sauce can also be used to make shrimp scampi or a nice chicken dish. If I want a meat sauce, I stir-fry some onion and hamburger then add a jar of sauce to it.

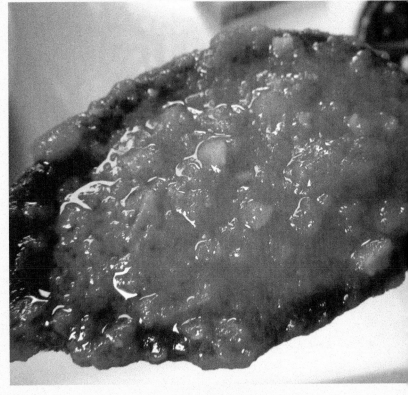

After heating, it can be served right away or (I prefer) refrigerated overnight to serve the next day. It's the best spaghetti meat sauce!

Remember, if it looks bad, smells bad or tastes bad, **DO NOT EAT IT!**

Chapter Eight

Fermentation

> It turns out that fermented foods not only provide digestive enzymes to help our guts but they also possess some formidable probiotics.

In the olden days, before we had electricity, one of the ways folks used to preserve their food was by fermenting. This process was easy to do, saved the bounty for future use and had some interesting side benefits. It turns out that fermented foods not only provide digestive enzymes to help our guts but they also possess some formidable probiotics. So all of the condiments that we used to ferment (mustard, ketchup, mayonnaise, pickles, sauerkraut and relishes) helped us to digest our food and protected us against bad bacteria.

It might be wise to return some of these items back into our menu planning. We don't even have to eat large amounts of these foods to gain some benefits. Certain people like the Koreans never gave this practice up (they wouldn't dream of eating a meal without their beloved kimchee—a sauerkraut-like condiment). Some even believe that fermented foods attack the plaque in our mouths. I can't say for sure, but I do know that—having sipped some beet kvass (a fermented beet drink) after all my meals for the past few years—my periodontist told me that all of my tooth pockets have become smaller than they were in previous years.

So I will share with you some of my favorite fermentation recipes. Most have the option of using whey.

Whey

You need raw milk to make whey. Pour some into a wide-mouth mason jar and leave it on the counter. It will stay there for four to seven days before it begins to separate. Once this occurs, pour it through cheesecloth in a strainer over a large bowl. The curds will stay in the cheesecloth and the whey drops through into the bowl. The curds can be used like cream cheese—add a few chives or dried basil and serve with crackers or veggies. Pour the whey into jars and keep it in the refrigerator. It keeps for several months.

> The curds will stay in the cheesecloth and the whey drops through into the bowl.

Beet Kvass

Beet kvass is actually a Ukranian drink. My husband, Bob, and I have gotten used to drinking a shot glass of it with all of our meals. I find it to be extremely tasty and refreshing.

Making beet kvass is easy. Use a quart mason jar and fill 1/4 to 1/3 with coarsely chopped raw beets. It's important to keep the beets chunky—grating them would cause the beets to create an alcoholic drink. Add one clove of fresh garlic (or a dried piece) and one teaspoon of salt. You can also add about 1/2 cup of homemade whey but this is an option and not completely necessary. Fill the jar with fresh filtered or well water (no chlorine or fluoride), leaving about an inch of "head space" (air) at the top. Secure the lid tightly while it brews on the kitchen counter for two days. It's important to shake the jar a few times each day but on the third day it gets put into the refrigerator. The flavor increases a bit if it is left in the refrigerator for a week or so before drinking, but is technically ready to go at this point.

Mayonnaise

Rolling the lemon around hard on the counter before slicing it increases the yield.

Good quality oils are often hard to come by in store-bought mayonnaise so it's nice to make your own. Using a food processor, start with three pastured chickens' egg yolks (again, make sure that they are disease-free), one tablespoon of fresh-squeezed organic lemon juice (rolling the lemon around hard on the counter before slicing it increases the yield), a bit of mustard, one tablespoon of homemade whey (optional), 1/4 teaspoon of turmeric, 1/4 teaspoon of cumin and a generous dash of salt. Pulse this combination for thirty seconds or so. Then add 3/4 cup of organic, cold-pressed and unrefined sunflower oil through the top of the food processor (almost drop by drop) while the mixture is spinning around. Funnel the mixture into a pint and a half jar and make a second batch to top it off. If using whey, it gets left on the counter overnight to ferment before putting it into the refrigerator. If you skip the whey, it goes right into the refrigerator.

Sauerkraut or Kimchee

In the fall, when carrots and cabbage are abundant, it's time to make a condiment that will last well into the winter. Slice one organic cabbage in your food processor and deposit it into a large sturdy mixing bowl. Add several organic grated carrots, one finely chopped organic onion, a few organic cloves of garlic, one teaspoon paprika powder, one tablespoon of salt and four tablespoons of homemade whey (optional). Take a heavy meat tenderizer and pound the mixture, turning it all around (I recommend wearing gloves so that you don't develop a blister on your hands). The goal is to get the juices flowing and the longer it gets pounded, the

103

The goal is to get the juices flowing and the longer it gets pounded, the more the juices come out.

more the juices come out. You might also consider using the same bowl from year to year as the pounding it takes does leave dents. Once this mix is pretty wet, start transferring it into a 1/2-gallon mason jar, being sure to pack it in as tight as you can get it. Stopping a few inches from the top, make sure that all of the mixture is under the brine; anything sticking up into the air can mold. Next, take a pint freezer bag and put a very small amount of water in it. Press the bag down on the kimchee all along the top to make sure the food stays under the brine. To keep the bag in place, put

a boiled (and cooled) rock on top. This jar is then covered tightly and left on the counter for about three days before moving it into the refrigerator. This mix is excellent in Reuben sandwiches.

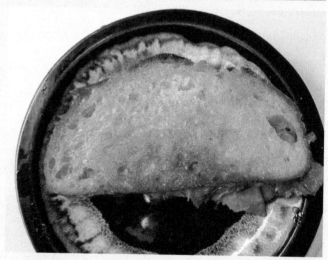

Fruit Kvass

Making fruit kvass is an incredibly easy way to add probiotics, vitamins, enzymes and beneficial yeasts to your diet. It can be made with any organic fruit or berries (using frozen berries or fruit is also fine). Vegetables can be added to the mix if you desire. Wash the fruit and, if it is large, like pineapple or apple, cut it into smaller pieces. If the fruit has a tough skin (like blueberries), mash them a little. Place in a 1/2-gallon jar. Add 1/4 teaspoon of salt and 1/4 cup of homemade whey can be added as well—this will help the kvass to last longer in the refrigerator but is not necessary. Fill the jar with pure water (well water or other water that does not contain chlorine or fluoride, etc.), leaving two inches of headspace or air at the top. Secure the lid tightly and cover with a towel. Leave on the kitchen counter for about two days, shaking often and opening the cover very briefly to release the gasses when you do (this will ensure that the mixture won't explode). At my house, it takes two days to ferment but it could take less or more time depending on the temperature in the kitchen. Look for small bubbles around the top of the jar and all the sweet taste to be gone, leaving only the essence of the fruit used and a slight effervescence. When done, pour the mix through a strainer. If you are in need of fiber, eat the fruit. Otherwise, this is not necessary. Place in the refrigerator and enjoy chilled.

If you are not used to ferments, begin drinking them slowly. It's important to introduce these bacteria into your digestive system gently so they won't cause problems. Introducing too much new bacteria into your gut can cause many individual cells to dump toxins into the bloodstream. While dumping toxins is a good thing, too many at once can make you feel terrible. Either water the kvass down or take very small servings to start. Look for great kvass recipes in Dr. Natasha Campbell-McBride's book, "Gut and Psychology Syndrome." Enjoy!

Ginger Ale

This is Sally Fallon Morell's recipe from "Nourishing Traditions" which she has generously given me permission to copy. It's a really refreshing drink that can be drunk in small amounts with meals or as a pick-me-up after work outside in the Sun.

Place the following ingredients in a two-quart jar:

3/4 cup ginger, peeled and finely chopped or grated
1/2 cup fresh lime juice
1/3 cup Rapadura or raw cane sugar
2 teaspoons sea salt
1/4 cup whey
2 quarts filtered water

Leaving two inches of headspace, or air at the top, stir well and cover tightly. Leave at room temperature for two to three days before transferring to the refrigerator. Well chilled, this will keep several months.

Remember if any food looks bad, smells bad or tastes bad - **DON'T EAT IT!**

Chapter Nine

Animals and Insects: Friends or Foes?

We share this planet with a plethora of other living beings. There is a delicate balance that has been created through millennia of interactions and sometimes the outcome lies in our favor while other times it does not. It's important to get to know which other life forms are helpful and which are not. The following is a small guide.

My Friends the Wasps

We have discussed in the other chapters the insects which plague some of my crops. However, there are some insects that are helpful—even very helpful—in the garden. We all know that bees pollinate many crops, and that praying mantises and ladybugs eat lots of different insects. However, few people realize the benefits that paper wasps bring to a vegetable patch; their favorite food is aphids. It is easy to tell when we bring a plant home from a nursery that has aphids as the wasps are all over it in minutes.

> It is easy to tell when we bring a plant home from a nursery that has aphids as the wasps are all over it in minutes.

Paper wasps are allowed to nest in spots that are out of the way around our house and in our greenhouse. They can't fly when the temperature is cool, so if we need to work near them, we do so in the early morning. When wasps end up in the house, we use a glass and a postcard to catch them and escort them back outside. We've been doing this for decades and the wasps almost look for the glass now.

I almost never get stung (not even once a year) but, when I do, I immediately pour some clear ammonia over the stinger to dissolve it.

Garden Foes

As much as we love our vegetables, there are lots of wild animals that love them too. Deer, rabbits, moles, chipmunks, mice and groundhogs can be a real problem. One of the best things that you can do to protect your crops is to put up a fence around the garden. As long as the fence is high enough and without holes, it should take care of the deer and rabbits. Having a dog that roams freely around the garden also helps

> One of the best things that you can do to protect your crops is to put up a fence around the garden.

to keep wild animals away. Wild animals know instinctively that they can't afford to be injured so they avoid domestic dogs and their environs.

Cats can be invaluable in keeping the mice and mole populations down. Of course, your cat would have to be a "mouser." If

you don't have a cat, mouse or rat traps are the next best thing for these pests. Mice seem to follow the same paths so if you catch one, you can usually catch lots more of them in this way. Bob says that peanut butter slathered on a well-secured prune usually works best. The only thing I have found that works for moles (and I've tried many options) is mole chasers. These metal whirligig-like windmills create sound vibrations that drive the moles away, as they have sensitive hearing. Whirligigs work as well, but they tend to fall apart as they are made of wood. The mole chasers are not cheap but seem strong enough to last for decades.

Groundhogs also can be a real problem. Luckily, we don't have them on our property because there is too much ledge for them to be able to tunnel. One way to get rid of this pest is to send them to "groundhog heaven" (shoot them). Of course, you will need to find out if your town has any ordinances concerning this activity first. You could also trap them and move them far, far away.

Chapter Ten

Backyard Chickens

At one time in the U.S., many families had some chickens. They were essential for providing eggs for breakfast and for baking. I believe that's why there are so many basic sayings in our language around chickens and their behavior. "Henpecked," "nest egg," "cocky," "don't put all of your eggs in one basket," "cooped up" and "don't count your chickens until they hatch" are merely a few of the dozens that we use on a regular basis.

As the Twentieth Century drew to a close, backyard chickens had almost disappeared from the American landscape. Cheap eggs were available from overcrowded barns and folks forgot what really good eggs tasted (and looked) like. But times have changed. The return of the backyard chickens is a terrific trend. Cities that formerly banned the keeping of these birds are changing their laws. The "good eggs" are back.

Chickens are relatively easy to keep. They don't need much room to be happy and the daily care can be done in minutes. The most important thing in this endeavor is to make sure that they are safe. Foxes, coyotes, fisher cats, raccoons, minks, bobcats, owls, hawks and many others in the "wild animal" category love chicken dinners. The coop must be sturdy and strong.

Properly building the coop and run are of primary importance. I am not going to try to write an entire treatise on keeping chickens here, but I will give a summary of what is necessary. It is well worth the effort.

> # The coop must be sturdy and strong.

If your land is flat and open, you might choose a moveable system called a "chicken tractor." This is a coop set up on wheels designed to be moved every few days with a tractor. It's a great way to give the chickens access to more bugs and grasses; you would need to provide an outside boundary with a moveable electric fence. This does not work, however, if you live in the woods or on ground that isn't relatively flat.

Due to space and land limitations, most people end up with a stationary coop. Some people start by pouring a slab of concrete and building up from there. Others put the coop on Sonotubes or telephone poles. We put ours on Sonotubes. It's nice because it gives the chickens room to play under the coop which stays free of rain and snow. Bear in mind that the floor and the rest of the coop need to be washable. Once a year, I take everything out of the coop (wearing a face mask) and wash it down with a hydrogen peroxide/water mix (about ten to twenty percent hydrogen peroxide). Everything gets cleaned. This has been essential in keeping our birds disease free.

The coop should also be located in partial shade, if possible. Chickens have a harder time with heat than they do with cold (they can fluff up their feathers after all). You want them to be able to lie in the Sun when they choose as this ensures that their eggs will contain some wonderful vitamin D, but you also want them to be able to get in the shade so they don't overheat. It's nice if the coop itself can remain cool. Chickens drink a lot more water in the summertime and some will even refuse to drink hot water—so choose your water location carefully.

> The door to the coop should also be sturdy and I recommend at least two closures (in case a predator is smart enough to figure out one of them).

Windows help to keep the summer air moving through the coop space. However, it's necessary to put hardware cloth (which is not a cloth at all, but a tightly woven, small spaces "fence") over all the windows to foil the predators. The door to the coop should also be sturdy and I recommend at least two closures (in case a predator is smart enough to figure out one of them). It's also handy to have a closet separate from the rest of the interior where you can keep the food and other gear.

Bob and I live in the woods so we made a permanent coop and run. We wanted our girls to have a lot of room in which to move so we fenced off a large area for them. The fence itself reaches about ten feet into the air (chickens can fly a little bit) in order to keep the birds inside. We also went around the entire bottom of the run with hardware cloth; it starts about three inches up onto the fence, and then is buried about eighteen inches outward under a few inches of soil. This is to stop the predators that like to dig under the fence to grab chickens.

For the flying predators (owls & hawks), we put some posts crowned with loops in the middle of the run with a piece of clothesline running through the loops from the top of the run to the bottom. We then took some surveyor's tape and crisscrossed the entire area every two feet from one side to the other. Any large bird would get their wings caught in this tape. We've had our chickens for six years and so far haven't lost one to a predator.

Inside the coop, the chickens need nesting boxes and a place to roost. It's nice to have the boxes on one side and the roosting posts on the other. Of course, they also need food and water containers. If you live in a cold climate, you will need the round electrical base which can keep the water warm when temperatures dip below freezing. We put a bit of insulation on the roof and made the structure quite tight (no drafts) so that even when we get low winter temperatures around 0°F, the chickens seem quite content.

We use wood shavings on the floor to help keep the coop clean and fresh. After several years of composting the chickens' poop mixed in with the wood shavings, we noticed that the wood shavings weren't breaking down in the compost but seemed to remain intact. A friend said that too much carbon was preventing it from breaking down. Another friend (who grew up on a chicken farm) suggested that we place something directly under the roosts to catch the chicken poop before it got mixed in with the shavings. So we now have several large, plastic, flat, rectangular boxes placed right under the roosts. I clean these boxes out on a regular basis and add the poop to the compost pile. The rest of the shavings get moved to a pile in the woods.

We give our chickens soy-free, organic feed or food that comes from a farmer that we know. They also get almost all of the weeds from the garden in the summer (which they love), kitchen scraps, fall leaves and winter hay. I add fresh-ground organic flax meal (to increase the good omegas) and kelp meal (for the trace minerals) to their feed. A calcium supplement is also necessary as well as grit.

> Chickens don't mind a light rain but they greatly dislike heavy rain and they hate snow.

Chickens don't mind a light rain but they greatly dislike heavy rain and they hate snow. They refuse to go outside when it is snowing. I generally grow some extra pumpkins and winter squashes to give them during these events so that they have something to peck at inside the coop besides each other. I also save my sunflower seeds

for the same purpose. Sometimes, if I am out of these, I get them a cabbage and chain it from the roost for them to peck. After the storm has passed, I shovel their ramp to the outside and create a little courtyard for them. I place hay around this courtyard so that they don't have to step directly on the snow and they enjoy pawing through it looking for seeds.

When the days get short and cold, chickens lay fewer eggs. The problem lies in the lack of light, not the colder weather. So I set up a light on a timer; it comes on at 4:00am and turns off at 7:00am. This allows the chickens to have a nice dark rest during the night followed by a nice extended daylight period. Chickens from large, factory farms are subjected to light 24/7 and never get to rest. When it is really, really cold (below 0°F), I turn on a heat lamp for them at night. Do be aware, though, that cobwebs are flammable. You would think that the chickens would eat all of the spiders but they don't. In the fall, I am always astounded at the amount of cobwebs clinging to just about every surface. I put on a face mask and knock them all down with a broom.

Chickens also molt once a year, meaning that they lose all of their feathers and grow new ones. This process can take several weeks to two months to complete and the girls lay few, if any, eggs during this time. Molting generally occurs in the late summer or early fall.

You can buy pullets ready to lay eggs from some nurseries, but these birds usually have had their beaks clipped (so that they won't peck at each other). This seems like a totally unnecessary and possibly cruel disfigurement since it interferes with their ability to forage and eat. Pullets can also be a bit unfriendly. It's better to get day-old chicks and raise them yourself. Of course, this requires a whole other list of items.

Mail order chicks arrive when they are a day or two old in the spring. I get mine at the beginning of May because they need to be kept warm and April can be quite cold where I live. My chicks stay on the porch in a large, black plastic horse-watering container. They are soft and fuzzy and absolutely adorable when they first arrive. The box will be cheeping away and everybody at the Post Office knows what's inside. I often ask that they give me a call ASAP when the chicks arrive so I can pick them up right away.

> It's easy to tell if the chicks are too cold (they all congregate right under the lamp) or too hot (none of them gets anywhere near the lamp).

Once home, I carefully lift out each chick, make it drink some water immediately and release it onto a double layer of paper towels that I have placed on the bottom of the container. I add some rocks to the opening of the waterer so that the chicks cannot fall in and drown. They are kept under a heat lamp with (preferably) a red light and the entire container is covered with blankets. The container needs to be about 95°F for the first few days (a thermometer is helpful). You can reduce this heat by about 5°F a week. It's easy to tell if the chicks are too cold (they all congregate right under the lamp) or too hot (none of them gets anywhere near the lamp). They need fresh water at all times. After a few days I add a layer of wood chips to the bottom of the container. At this time, it's often best to raise the waterer onto a few bricks. Otherwise, the chips get into it and foul the water.

One problem that is common with baby chicks is called "pasty butt." The chick's poop will dry right on its little butt and this literally blocks it from being able to eliminate. If you don't get it off, the chick will die. I fill a small

container with warm
water and immerse
the butt into it until
it dissolves. I use a
paper towel to remove
the residue and place
the chick back in the
container. Depending
on when you get your
chicks, they need to be
in this brooder for six
to twelve weeks. They
are ready to move when

they have developed feathers and the weather outside is fairly warm.

Baby chicks cannot be placed in a coop with full-sized chickens. You will
need a separate coop for them (and run) until they are as big as the older
chickens. They will be eating different food as well. Their coop needn't have
nesting boxes but they will need roosts. We used a plastic calf's shed and put
hardware cloth over the windows and (VERY importantly) under the shed.
Again, think anti-predator. We put this shed on the inside edge of the big girls'
run then erected a separated chicken wire run for them. All the chickens can
see each other, but the little ones are protected from the big ones (who would
eat them).

Chickens lay eggs quite well for the first two years. After that, it is more
sporadic. We keep our hens until they are two and beginning to molt and then
make them into stew birds. For this reason, I get different breeds each year
so that I know which ones are the older chicks without having to mark them
individually. You can't bake these old girls as they have strong, hard muscles
which are tough. However, cooking them in water for a long period of time
(all day) in the crock pot or on low on the stovetop renders a delicious and
nutritious meal. I always add an onion right away as onions bring out the
flavor of meat. Beets, carrots, potatoes, mushrooms, broccoli or any other
vegetable can be added an hour or two before the meal.

Chapter Eleven

Some Additional Ways to Save Money

Composting

Composting is easy and results in lots of free goodies for the vegetable and flower gardens. Everyone with a yard should do it. Many gardening catalogues and stores offer lots of different kinds of barrels, pails, pyramids, tumblers, wood slated or cedar bins, or wheeled or raised composters. Ideally, to make compost quickly, it is best to be able to turn the pile easily. However, if you put the right kind of stuff in the compost pile, it will eventually break down even if you ignore it.

My compost pile is a 5'x5'x5' garden fence bin. Chicken wire also works well. There are posts at the corners where the fencing is attached. I have two compost bins and I rotate between them, dumping into one until it is quite full, and then resting it for at least a year while dumping into the other one. After a year of rest, I bring the compost to my garden. It generally looks like deep, brown, rich earth and is often loaded with earthworms. It would be better if I had three bins; one to dump into, one to cook and one to put back into the garden. The plants absolutely love it.

> Much of what most people throw away can be added to a compost pile.

Much of what most people throw away can be added to a compost pile. Most kitchen scraps, shredded leaves, hay, coffee wastes, nutshells, eggshells, unbleached paper towels and weeds from the garden all make excellent compost. If your weeds have already gone to seed, however, you may want to put them in a different place—otherwise, you will be replanting them into the garden. I solved this problem for myself by feeding the weeds to the chickens. Then, I can put the chicken manure (sans seeds) into the compost pile. You also want to avoid putting the debris from any diseased plants into the pile as you don't want to reintroduce the pathogens back into the garden. Smelly stuff like meat, fish and dairy should be avoided as well.

Re-use, Re-use, Re-use

An integral part of sustainability comes from utilizing our resources in as many ways as possible. At our house, we re-use anything that we can. Boxes sent to us from mail-order businesses get recycled to mailing shops. When we mail order frozen foods, the empty containers get dropped off at a friend's farm next to an Inn and reused by folks who like to bring home their pastured meats. Glass jars are especially precious as we fill them with homemade spaghetti sauce, jams, pickles, sauerkraut, dried herbs, garlic powder and paprika powder. Plastic bags get reused as many times as they can stand. Kitchen scraps go to the chickens or the compost pile and we have bins to recycle tins and glass (that we can't reuse). Sponges get bleached every few days (ten percent solution) instead of using throw-away wipes.

Most towns now offer recycling for many things including cardboard, newspapers and magazines. Some areas even have composting available. Be active to ensure that your town is among the ones thinking ahead.

Indoor Drying Rack

I have never owned a clothes dryer. In the summer, I hang my clothes outside on the line where they blow in the breeze and absorb the sweetest of smells. I realize that this is not possible for some people—building associations often forbid it. However, there is an indoor option that I utilize in the winter

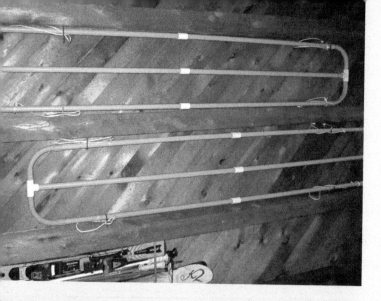

that could possibly be used year round; I use a clever drying rack that my husband, Bob, built me. The clothes dry in no time at all and the moisture is a welcome addition to our indoor air. It was unbelievably inexpensive to build and it also is a money-saver.

Bob got some schedule 40 electrical conduit (he does say he might use schedule 80 for strength if he were to do it again). As you can see by the picture, he glued these pieces together in a large rectangle creating three long drying surfaces. I scrubbed the writing off of the schedule 40. It hangs down on bits of clothesline that are attached to the beams and lives up under the ceiling on nails and hooks that are attached to the sides of the beams. It's unobtrusive and quite handy. Clothes, towels and sheets will dry overnight so it doesn't have to be a nuisance during the day. I highly recommend it.

> The clothes dry in no time at all and the moisture is a welcome addition to our indoor air.

A Solar Oven

Solar Cooking International's mission is to spread solar thermal cooking technology to benefit people and environments. They help underprivileged people in sunny environments not only to be able to cook their food but also to pasteurize water for drinking. I have a solar oven which works wonderfully in the summertime. Who wants to heat up their kitchen when it's hot? And the fuel is free! For more information, go to solarcookers.org.

The Rain Barrel

Water is an essential element in maintaining a garden. One way to save money and energy for watering the garden is to keep a rain barrel. We put a gutter on the downward side of our wood/garden shed and funnel the rain into a fifty-gallon drum. Bob put a spigot on the bottom of our drum and it's easy to get the water out of the rain barrel. I use it to water the garden, clean my shoes after spending time in the chicken run and clean the chickens' nesting boxes when we get a broken egg. It's extremely handy and doesn't use one iota of any kind of power source. Do check with local authorities, though, before installing a rain barrel. Some states don't allow them. The NCSL (National Conference of State Legislatures) shows rainwater/grey water harvesting regulations online. Most extreme regulations occur where water is scarce. Some states actually offer financial incentives for them.

Chapter Twelve

Other Voices

Many people in my community and, indeed, across the country are working to restore a more natural harmony to our planet. I wanted to share some of their thoughts and voices. The following represents my conversations with these industrious individuals.

Soil Consultant, Tim Wightman

Tim Wightman is a soil consultant who travels all over the country giving lectures to many different farm groups and providing soil assessments for all types of farms. He helped me in my garden and if you follow his advice, will undoubtedly help you with yours.

Celeste: Why is soil health so important?

Tim: Because it is the basis of all life. Our soil has been badly neglected. We've taken from it but have never given back or even been cognizant of what our soil needs to provide the proper nourishment for our food.

Celeste: How can people replace these minerals?

Tim: The most important thing people need to know is what type of soil they have to start with. The only way to do this is to have the soil tested (county extension agents can give you directions on how to do this and where to send it). Soil has finite parameters—it needs to be balanced properly in order to work well. You don't want to upset the system. Improperly balanced soil can shut down and stop growing many things.

Celeste: Is there an ideal formula for compost?

Tim: No, not really. There is never only one thing that will work to cover all the needs of the soil. It's a combination of a lot of things. Compost is part of a fertility program (management of the soil). It is only as good as the source from which it came. It can be made from many different things, but generally only carries a limited amount of certain trace minerals or macrominerals like phosphorus or potassium. For this reason, you have to know your source as well as the plants that you are planting. Basically, with a small garden, there are only two distinct groups of plants—ones that set fruit and ones that don't. Plants that do not set fruit need more phosphorus and a wee bit more nitrogen. Plants that set fruit need more potassium and calcium. Compost won't carry these minerals unless somebody puts them in. If you're looking to build up your soil, compost is good, but too much compost creates its own issues. The rule is everything in moderation when you're working with the soil. It also takes a while to balance out the soil once you add something, so you have to go slow. You can always add more of something to compost, but you can't take it back.

> Soil has finite parameters—it needs to be balanced properly in order to work well.

Celeste: You made a comment to me once that you believe that without ruminants, we wouldn't survive.

Tim: Yes, everybody is worried about the bees right now and rightly so because the bees do the pollination. However, it's the ruminants we have on this Earth that help build the soil. Ruminants are animals with a rumen, a four-chambered stomach, such as your goats, sheep, beef and dairy cows. If you are going to use manure, you want to get it from ruminants because they are the fermentation vats of soil microbes. The rumen microbes that break down the food for the ruminants are the same microbes that exist in the soil. It's the same set of bacteria that work on the parameters of calcium, phosphorus, potassium and trace minerals. Many of the pro- and pre-biotics sold today that are designed to improve a person's stomach and digestive system, are made from soil bacteria called colony forming bacteria. We're in the process of learning that humans are dependent on the same microbes that work with the earthworms and come from ruminants. Ruminants actually leave behind in their manure untold numbers of microbes. Everything is in place so the microbes have something to do for the plants who feed them. In its microbial mix, it has the proper amount of starch to break down straw or dying plant material, phosphorus, calcium and all the trace minerals that the microbes are very dependent upon.

> If you are going to use manure, you want to get it from ruminants because they are the fermentation vats of soil microbes.

Celeste: Another thing that you told me once was that you can tell the health of tomato plants by their leaves.

Tim: There are several reasons why leaves curl, but sometimes, if the leaves are curled up on the sides, then that means there's a lack of potassium. And, often, if the leaf tips are curled back underneath themselves, then that means there's a lack of calcium.

Celeste: What do you think of foliar sprays (foliar sprays are a way to get nutrients into plants by spraying mineralized water onto the leaves early or late in the day)?

Tim: Foliars are great; you just have to understand which foliar products to use. Many common quick-fix products will show immediate results but over time will unbalance the soil. When you use foliar sprays you are actually feeding the plants through their leaves. This can work really well except for calcium, which I believe has to come directly from the soil. Using foliar sprays helps speed up the process of building soil because the plant now has excess sugars and nutrients from food-born microbes and does not need to get all of its nutrients from the soil. I recommend using micronized foliar applications which means the phosphorus, potassium, cobalt, magnesium and other contents are ground very, very fine. This way, the plant doesn't have to use its sugars to break these minerals down to utilize the microbes. It's already broken down.

> When you use foliar sprays you are actually feeding the plants through their leaves.

Celeste: Anything you would like to add?

Tim: When people work with soil, they have to move slowly. It's not an immediate gratification thing. It has its own timeframe. If you understand that, it will reward you with a great garden. But, if you try too hard for quicker results, you'll hurt yourself in the long run. As with conventional agriculture, a quick fix won't solve the problem, it only addresses the symptom. It takes years to get truly healthy soil that produces healthy plants.

> If a plant has the right nutrition, it should have a good defense system.

Celeste: When plants are harmed by insects, isn't that a sign that the soil isn't right?

Tim: If a plant has the right nutrition, it should have a good defense system. It will be really high in sugar and I believe no insect can eat a high sugar plant. The only reason that we have diseases and pests is because the plants are not healthy.

Community Garden Creators,
Nick Zachary and Fritze Till

Nick Zachary and Fritze Till are two teachers and Walpole, NH residents who created a local community garden. It is a huge success and donates much food to the elderly and the food bank. I wanted to find out how they did it.

Celeste: What is the most important thing to know about setting up a community garden?

Nick: It's a community effort (a group that works together for the common good) and it's about openness. It's the vision that you have and the tone that you set with the people. We're all going to learn from each other.

Fritze: You really have to want to do a garden. You can't just have some vision because it's trendy; you have to want, in yourself, to do this community

project. Otherwise it's impossible to get other people inspired. People are looking for someone to guide them. You also have to be open about how it's going to work and be willing to listen to everyone's ideas.

Nick: We also physically participated. We volunteered and spent time with people. We helped take care of things while people were away. We led by example.

Celeste: If somebody wanted to start a community garden, how would they go about finding a space?

Fritze: First of all, think about what a garden requires—the site itself—and think about whom you are going to serve. Will it be easily accessible? What resources are you going to need? You have to find a space that can adapt to your needs. There are a lot of things to contemplate when picking the right location.

Nick: Ask around. Churches sometimes have land, or the town, or schools. Or buildings with flat roofs upon which a garden could be created. Senior centers are another option—you could make beds that were really high so that people in chairs could garden. There are a lot of places.

Fritze: Remember to look closely at things. One community garden I know of was getting their water from the town which they thought was great, except it was full of fluoride which is very hard on plants. It is important to ask questions ahead of time. Where are the water, manure, and building materials going to come from? For us, soil amendments have been our greatest outlay. Local donations of manure and compost helped us the first few years. However, in order to be fair to the farmers, we've decided to have an annual fee to help pay for these items.

Nick: The other thing to remember is that we have been donating tons and tons of food to the local food pantry.

Fritze: Probably twenty percent of what we grow goes to our food pantry and senior housing. Feeding people is definitely part of our mission and that will continue.

> Probably twenty percent of what we grow goes to our food pantry and senior housing.

Nick: There's a town in Connecticut where about an acre of fire department land is used for a large community garden. The fire department put water lines under the ground and they have a couple of spigots coming up to water the garden. If you have a community garden concept where you will be donating to senior centers or food pantries, people are likely to come forward and help.

Fritze: When folks want to donate, I have to think about the consequences. When someone wanted to donate alpaca poop, then horse, we said yes to alpaca and no to horse. Horses are not ruminants; the very best soil bacteria come from ruminants. This is where specificity is really important.

Nick: It really helps to be a visionary and attract folks who want to work to be self-sufficient.

Fritze: We aim for zero waste and we compost everything except stuff that would attract predators. One thing that has brought us together as a group is a weekly email during the growing season. It's not instructional but observational. We discuss garlic shoots coming up in the spring or bird sightings or plan group dinners.

Nick: Something that really worked in our garden is to spend time with newcomers.

Fritze: Gardens are really so basic, it eludes people. What is more basic than putting food in your mouth?

Celeste: Gardening and food preservation are things that many of our great grandparents knew. They wouldn't have dreamed of not having a garden.

Fritze: And, it's not just in the US. I was talking to some old fella in a tiny village in Spain and he said, "We are the last generation who are going to know how to grow food." And he was working in his garden.

Celeste: Talk to me a bit about your watering system.

Nick: The water is downhill from the garden. Luckily a local electrician provided a pump and every spring we bring a hose down to the pond with a one-way valve. The water comes up from the pond and goes through a four-way splitter. At the top of the hill, we have three 275-gallon tanks. During the growing season, whenever anyone wants water, they run the pump and they fill the three tanks. Everybody is trained on how to use this system. So when the pump is pumping, we can fill any or all of the tanks. Then we gravity feed it into the garden.

Fritze: The water itself is coming out of a wetland that is nutrient-dense.

Nick: When you're using the water, you can smell the decaying matter, so that's a good system. It's like compost water. The tanks are recycled from a local company. They sit up on platforms so the water comes out gravity-fed. Each of the tanks has a splitter on them so now that we have three tanks, six people can be watering at once.

> The water itself is coming out of a wetland that is nutrient-dense.

Celeste: How many people are in the community garden now?

Nick & Fritze: Twenty-six. We still have room for a few more.

Fritze: I've actually been visiting other community gardens and they are all different. It depends on your community needs.

Rooftop Tower Garden Farmer, Joy Kelly

Chapala Gardens is a rooftop farm in Santa Barbara, CA owned by husband and wife team, Sandy Campbell and Joy Kelly. Their daughter, Jake Kelly, manages it. The garden is comprised completely of Tower Gardens— aeroponic towers that allow almost a ton of produce to be harvested annually from this small rooftop space. I spoke with Joy Kelly about the farm and the towers.

Celeste: Tell us a bit about your business.

Joy: We are technically a farm. We are able to grow most of the produce for the entire community that we live in—our West Beach community of Santa

Barbara. We use aeroponic technology, not hydroponic. This is even more sustainable than hydroponic. It uses less water and nutrients; there is no waste because it's a closed-loop system and the units that we use last a lifetime (they don't have to be replaced like much of the hydroponic materials do). The food that we grow is also quite healthy.

Celeste: Why did you choose that aeroponic system?

Joy: We weren't actually looking to start a farm. We own a triplex down on the beach in Santa Barbara; we rent two and live in the other one. We've been working for the Juice Plus+®.company for the last nineteen years. Their commitment is to get people to eat more fruits and vegetables. One of the best ways to get people to do this is to get them to grow some vegetables. We had a lot of gardening programs, but not everyone can become a soil gardener. Even though I grew up with a mom who gardened, I was sometimes successful and sometimes not. I think some years I had the world's most expensive tomatoes because of how little production I got out of them. Juice Plus+® is really a product introduction company. In forty-three years we've introduced five products, with the Tower Garden being the fifth one. If our president thinks that a product is going to make a big difference in everyone's quality of life, he will feature it. When he saw the towers, he was instantly taken. Not only is this an easy and efficient way to grow things, but (especially here in California with our tremendous drought) it fits our need to change the way we grow food.

> Not only is this an easy and efficient way to grow things, but (especially here in California with our tremendous drought) it fits our need to change the way we grow food.

Celeste: Explain how the towers work.

Joy: They are really simple. They were developed at the Epcot Center in Orlando, FL. Juice Plus+® bought the concept from Tim Blank who developed them.

There's a twenty-gallon reservoir on the bottom and there's a small twenty-watt pump (like a fish tank pump) which also resides at the bottom. Its energy use is quite small. It's set on a timer—we normally have it on for fifteen minutes and off for fifteen minutes. At night, we could have it come on only once every couple of hours, but we leave it on for the fifteen-minute routine all the time. It costs about seventy cents a month to run a pump out here (in California) which pumps water and nutrients up to the top of the column. The towers can be anywhere from five to eleven tiers high. We don't recommend eleven for household use, but each tier holds four plants. Our farm does have some towers with eleven tiers. So, in five square feet of space, we can grow forty-four huge heads of kale or lettuce. We also grow tomatoes, squashes, beans and snow peas. Each level is designed to get hit evenly with the water and nutrients as it moves

So, in five square feet of space, we can grow forty-four huge heads of kale or lettuce.

down. There are little baskets that hold the plants. We check the pH once a week and we add nutrients every other time we add water. The towers need to be cleaned but we use reverse osmosis water which is pretty free of mineral buildup so we only need to clean them out every three to four months. If we used hard water, we'd probably need to clean them every six to eight weeks. That's about it!

> They found that the nutrient content when harvested is equal but plants in the tower gardens grow thirty percent bigger in 2/3 of the time. It's a much more efficient way to grow.

Chapala Gardens started off with two towers and we liked them so much that we went to six. But once we realized that we could make a difference in the sustainability of our community and our food security, we put forty of them on our roof. It's really a lovely place to be.

Celeste: You can grow anything but root crops in the towers?

Joy: We can grow anything but root crops, trees or bushes. We encourage people when they are first starting, to get good at growing greens—lettuce, kale and arugula. Things that need to be pollinated can be a little trickier for people when they first start. Once they get the hang of the greens, they can grow other foods they would like. The greens can actually survive down to about 27°F. Last year, there was a point where we were the only farmers at the farmers' market that had lettuce.

Celeste: What goes into the water?

Joy: We put the tower tonic into the water with 100 different earth and sea minerals. You could also use fish emulsion or compost tea; whatever you would like to use. The University of Mississippi has done studies on the tower tonic comparing plants grown this way to produce grown with some very best soil. They found that the nutrient content when harvested is equal but plants in the tower gardens grow thirty percent bigger in 2/3 of the time. It's a much more efficient way to grow.

4-H Leader, Holly Gowdy

Holly Gowdy and her husband, Christian, run Brookfield Farm, a small, local, grass-fed animal farm in Walpole, NH. They raise beef cattle, dairy cattle, goats and sheep. They participate in Walpole's Farmers' Market and have farm store hours on Saturdays or by appointment. They can be reached at cdgowdyco@aol.com or at 603.445.5104.

Celeste: What is 4-H?

Holly: 4-H is an organization for youth development to help kids learn.

Celeste: Agricultural stuff?

Holly: Anything. That's what makes 4-H different from other youth development organizations. Each state has its own land grant university. In New Hampshire it's the University of New Hampshire. Most land grant universities have a cooperative extension office in every county within their state. There is a 4-H educator in those offices who finds and trains

> And what really makes the program unique is the educational process that trains its volunteers so that they are really good at what they teach...

volunteers to work with the kids. And what really makes the program unique is the educational process that trains its volunteers so that they are really good at what they teach, whether it be agriculture, cooking or gardening. They even have programs in robotics and sciences. So essentially, if you have children with an interest and you have an adult volunteer who is willing to be screened and educated on how to teach that interest, you have a 4-H club.

133

I actually started in 4-H when I was eight and lived in Connecticut. My family relocated a couple of times to other states, but there was always a 4-H club that I could plug into.

Celeste: You said that you started a 4-H club?

Holly: The Walpole area has benefited from the Pinnacle View 4-H Club for over sixty years, but their focus had always been solely on dairy cattle. When I moved here, there were some kids that were interested in dealing with beef cattle—a different way of raising cows. Because Christian and I were raising beef cattle and they knew that I was a 4-H person, they asked if I would help those kids. So that is how I became a 4-H volunteer.

I switched to teaching about sheep because my son and some of his friends became interested in them. Because sheep are so different than cows, the cooperative extension educator said to create our own 4-H club. We could get together with the Pinnacle View 4-H on big projects, but also work on our own. So we started the Great River 4-H Club this last fall (2013).

Celeste: How do you start a 4-H club?

Holly: First you need at least three or four kids with a strong interest in something like raising chickens or growing vegetables. There has to be a goal. If you have kids that don't know what they want to do, you have no direction. You should also have two adult volunteers. With most 4-H Clubs, there's a business meeting once a month. There also needs to be an elected slate of officers. The club name is chosen by ballot.

In our 4-H Club, the kids decide what types of projects they want to do. We had a number of kids interested in sheep and a smaller number who were interested in poultry. Together they are a big group (sheep kids and chicken kids); there's about eighteen of them. At the monthly meetings, the sheep kids talk about sheep stuff and the chicken kids talk about chicken stuff. During the course of the month, the group might meet two or three times. If there are any related activities in the state of New Hampshire, we try to figure out how to go and participate. The chicken kids all went to the Big E (a large regional fair in Massachusetts) last year.

There needs to be an educated person to teach the different curriculums. The cooperative extensions have lots of nice resources including curriculum books that show people how to teach a subject. These are all available for free through their lending library. Then there are county activities that bring all the county kids together. There is a 4-H Day in April. This year it's a communications focus with a photography contest and my son is going to do a demonstration on waxing cross country skis (even though that is not the focus of his 4-H group). That's the beauty of it—there are no set rules as long as the kids put it together themselves and present it themselves. These contests begin at the county level and, if the child does well, can go to a state level, then a big regional level. The older kids can go as far as the national level in Louisville, Kentucky.

> It's also a way for kids who prefer hands-on learning to book learning to excel.

Celeste: Do they get prizes?

Holly: They get a ribbon. To me, the benefit comes from kids learning and getting better and better at what they do. It's also a way for kids who prefer hands-on learning to book learning to excel.

Environmental Teacher, Eloise Clark

Eloise Clark was instrumental in getting a grant from the National Resource Conservation Service (NRCS) to build a high tunnel (a type of unheated, solar greenhouse) at the local, Walpole, NH. elementary school. The kids plant the gardens, care for them and bring the harvest in to the lunch ladies. I wanted to find out how she got the grant.

Celeste: Who do you work for?

Eloise: I work for the Frederick H. Hooper Institute in Walpole, NH.

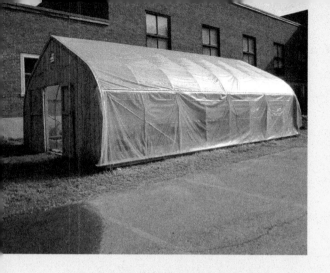

Celeste: What is that?

Eloise: It's a town education program where we go into Walpole schools and teach the children about agriculture, forestry, soils and environmental science.

Celeste: Why do you think that it's important for kids to learn this?

Eloise: These are all life skills. Learning the stewardship of the Earth is very important. The children learn about their neighborhoods, the land and the soil, and thus become more connected to their home. It's also a chance for them to get away a bit from the world of electronics.

Celeste: What kinds of things do you do with the kids?

Eloise: People from the Hooper Institute go into the classrooms one day a week. There are some school gardens (some that were already there and some new ones since installing the high tunnel) that the kids are taught to work in. In the sixth grade, there is a unit on forestry that takes about half a year. I go into the classrooms once a week and start with tree identification, then forest ecology and management. For the fifth grade, I focus a lot on animals and wildlife. The sessions start with insects in the fall, then migration, predator and prey, endangered species, reptiles and amphibians and it finishes with birds in the spring. For the fourth grade, the kids go out to various farms or forestry operations. They visit a sawmill, a wood-turning shop, a dairy farm, a horse farm, a Christmas tree plantation, an apple orchard and watch haymaking and maple sugaring. They get to see the people at work, ask questions and then document it. Because it is difficult to take whole classrooms on field trips, much of the teaching is done at the schools. That's one reason we brought the gardens to the schools.

Celeste: Where was the first garden that you did?

Eloise: It was at the Walpole Primary School. My colleague, Fritze Till, started it with the K-3 kids. There are eight or nine beds. My current colleague, Rebecca Whippie, has maintained it and kept it going through the years with the kids.

Celeste: Do they eat the food?

Eloise: Yes, that's the tricky part; to grow things that the students can eat at the edges of the growing season because they are not there for two months in the summer. So you have to get your peas in really early.

Celeste: And, in the fall?

Eloise: In the fall, there's a lot of stuff waiting for them when they get back from summer break. We do a lot of herbs and squashes and beets.

Celeste: Greens?

Eloise: We've done greens more up at the middle school. We have a high-tunnel greenhouse there that was just established this year (a high tunnel is an unheated—except by the Sun—greenhouse which allows people in cold climates to extend their growing season). We received funding from the Cheshire County Conservation District

> Yes, that's the tricky part; to grow things that the students can eat at the edges of the growing season because they are not there for two months in the summer.

which is part of the NRCS which is under the wing of the USDA. The NRCS is a federal program that works with private landowners to make conservation improvements to their land. The NRCS offered grant opportunities for high tunnels on public land. I happened to be on the board of the Cheshire County Conservation District which is the public face of the NRCS and I thought, "this is something that I could do." So I alerted quite a few schools in our county. I then wrote a grant with the help of Glen Stan, the guidance counselor from the Walpole Middle School, and we were awarded funding for the high tunnel.

Celeste: Did you have a lot of volunteers to help build the high tunnel?

Eloise: Yes. We used the middle school students when we could—using hand tools—but we couldn't let them use any power tools. We had a lot of parents and one man who had done this before. There were also folks who were experienced with general building principles. It was nice to have some experienced people helping out. We adults did the raising of the ribs (setting up the framing) in one day but the kids did most of the pounding of the stakes (which took considerably longer).

> The kids decided that they didn't like chard that much until the lunch lady steamed it and put cheese on it.

Celeste: What do you plant in the high tunnel?

Eloise: This fall, we planted lettuce, chard, spinach and collards. It was a little slow to start but, by the end of October, it began to take off. We fill up some really large bowls a couple of times a week. I made a field guide of the greens; I took pictures of them all and made posters. The kids decided that they didn't like chard that much until the lunch lady steamed it and put cheese on it. When it got really cold, I put another piece of plastic on some ribs over the beds and the lettuce, chard, spinach and collards made it through the whole Christmas vacation. We picked another huge bowl when we got back to school.

Celeste: If somebody else wanted to build a high tunnel, would they contact the NRCS directly?

Eloise: Yes. They could find out where their local conservation district is and contact them. There should be some funds available for high tunnels.

Celeste: Anything else that you would like to recommend?

Eloise: Yes, I would definitely like to recommend the UNH Cooperative Extension's Junior Master Gardener's Program. It has lots of good information about gardening and it details how to teach it. It's been well tested. Folks from any state could get the guide books by calling 888.900.2577 or by going to the JMG website at www.jmgkids.us/.

Or, other states may have their own programs. Any kind of cooperative extension which is part of a state's university system can be very helpful. Many will do soil tests for you. You don't have to reinvent the wheel. There's a lot of information out there.

Farmstay Innkeeper, Jackie Caserta

Jackie Caserta has a beautiful bed and breakfast in the heart of Walpole Valley Farms in Walpole, NH. She's been in the innkeeping business for fourteen years, has won a number of distinctive awards (including named one of New England's Best Historic Inns by Yankee Magazine and recognized as a 2011 New Hampshire Farm of Distinction) and has developed a loyal following. Her B&B is different from most as it is located right in the middle of a beautiful farm. Guests get to join in with chores or just observe. You can see pictures of her farm at innatvalleyfarms.com or contact her at 603.756.2855. If you'd like to experience life on the farm, consider a stay with her or any farmstay at farmstayus.org.

Celeste: Why do people come for a farmstay?

Jackie: The number one type of guest we have are families with young children. When calling, people often tell me they want to give their children the farm experience as a pretense. Once they get here though, more often than not, it's the adults that are just as interested. I mention this because I'll be in the garden pulling carrots with a family and after the initial newness wears off the kids are perfectly happy to be swinging on the swings, but I can't get the adults out of the garden – they want to see and taste everything!

Celeste: Maybe they want to be part of a farm so that they can learn how to teach their children?

Jackie: That's a big part of it, but most of our guests come from the city and they don't think they have a place to garden. They often don't realize how much they can produce even with just a front lawn. Some of them had the experience as children visiting their grandparents' farm before it was sold. They long for that memory of a connection to family and roots and history. They miss it. They also want their children to have a similar experience. We have a lot of guests in their late twenties and early thirties who are really into fresh, local food and want to understand it more. Farmstays are relatively new in this country so people don't really know what to expect. Here guests can choose to have a farmstay experience or not. Some folks just want to stay at the Inn and look out the window at the bucolic setting while asking questions at the breakfast table while others insist on helping and getting their hands dirty.

It's up to the guests how much or how little they want to participate.

Celeste: If someone comes specifically for a farmstay, what do you offer them?

Jackie: It's up to the guests how much or how little they want to participate. We offer walking tours of our farm to all of our guests during their stay where we visit the farm animals, talk about the history of the farm and our sustainable farming practices, walk through our no-till gardens, collect eggs, etc. Guests that come as families will often stay in our cottages which have full kitchens so they have the ability to cook. We have extensive gardens so guests cannot only go visit the animals and collect farm fresh eggs, but they can pick produce, herbs and edible flowers and go back into the cottage and cook a meal with the food they've collected. Our farm-raised, grass-fed

140

meats are also available for sale in our farm store. Guests get to see, feel, taste, touch and talk to us for a complete experience, from start to finish. We walk through the garden and teach them what different plants look like when they're growing (as opposed to packed in cellophane in the grocery store) and they get really excited about it. Some guests take things a step further and ask to participate in some physical aspect of farming that they want to learn about like harvesting, weeding, fencing, chicken processing, etc.

For those guests just looking for a place to stay they often only want to talk about fresh local food, organics and the like over breakfast. Each morning I make a three-course farm-to-table breakfast from scratch using as much as I can that comes right from our farm so food quickly gets the conversation started. "Why are these eggs yolks so dark orange?" "I've never tasted eggs this good!" "How did you cook them?" These are just a few of the questions/ comments I hear often. My answers are always the same: "When you start with fresh quality ingredients and cook simply you can hardly go wrong – let the food speak for itself." Sometimes green heirloom tomatoes get left on the plate until I explain that the Zebra variety is ripe when green. This will often lead to a discussion of heirloom tomatoes. For some guests this is all the experience they want.

Celeste: Isn't there an organization for farmstays?

Jackie: Farmstayus.org is an organization of farmstays across the U.S. It was started by a woman, Scottie Jones, at Leaping Lamb Farm in Oregon. She's recently begun structuring the organization into a nonprofit so she can go after grant funding and partnerships that will help bring the message of farmstays to Americans. Each farmstay is really different. Leaping Lamb Farm raises sheep and offers one cottage for on-farm lodging, while others are dairy, alpaca or horse farms with accommodations for many more guests.

Celeste: What do you have at Walpole Valley Farms?

Jackie: We have one hundred percent grass-fed beef and lamb, pasture-raised chickens and turkeys and foraging pigs. We raise full-size meat chickens and egg layers as well as Bantam chickens and cashmere goats. We also raise small fruits including strawberries, raspberries, and blueberries as well as a wide variety of produce, edible flowers and herbs. We have a high

So we can have the conversation inside over our farm-to-table breakfast and then go outside and show people what we're talking about.

tunnel which is a passive solar greenhouse. Growing cold-hardy vegetables in a high tunnel allows us to harvest fresh food nearly year-round without the use of any fossil fuels. Our ever-bearing strawberries supply us from the first week of May until the second week of November. So we can have the conversation inside over our farm-to-table breakfast and then go outside and show people what we're talking about.

A lot of times, people say this is great, but that they can't afford to buy organic. You don't have to buy all organic. Start with one or two things that are important to you. It also doesn't have to be certified organic. Go to the farmers' market and find out who your farmers are. For many years, we were certified organic. But, between the cost of the certification process and the fact that I'm really not selling anything (I mostly grow food to feed my family and to share with my guests), the cost of the certification process didn't make sense for us. If you follow all the organic standards and sell less than $5,000 annually you can still call yourself organic, just not certified organic. We actually go over and beyond the standards as do many other small local farmers. There's currently no "label" for this type of food production so you don't know unless you ask. If you're buying food at a local farm stand or farmers' market you could already be buying organic and simply not know it.

Celeste: So it doesn't have to be labeled organic?

Jackie: If you're buying in the grocery store it does, but, in my opinion, when you're buying local, it doesn't. There are plenty of other people in our community that grow vegetables and fruits without the use of chemical fertilizers and pesticides that could qualify for organic or nearly so. The important thing is to go to your farmers' market and meet your farmers and ask them how they grow their produce and raise their animals for their meats. If they are not transparent (and most farmers are), shop elsewhere. Often farmers have a store at their farm, a pick-your-own at the end of the season and/or offer seconds (slightly damaged goods), all options to get fresh, great quality, clean food for very reasonable cost. Almost every farm—at the abundance of the season—offers bulk rates. It might take a little more time than shopping at a chain grocery store, but there's value in spending an afternoon at a farm with your family getting some exercise and fresh air, developing a relationship with a local farmer, creating memories and making connections with the land all while supporting your local economy. It's hard to put a price tag on the value of all that. You also have to factor in the health and environmental benefits—there is much higher nutrition from fresh, local fruits and vegetables and grass-fed meats than processed foods that travel thousands of miles to get to your plate. Then you put some of that great fresh food away in the freezer to help feed you in the winter. Not only is it a cost savings, but commercially prepared food doesn't taste the same. Every time I buy fresh corn on the cob in season, I buy two dozen and cook them both. We eat one dozen right away, then I cut the rest off of the cob and I put it in the freezer. It's very simple and easy.

> You also have to factor in the health and environmental benefits—there is much higher nutrition from fresh, local fruits and vegetables and grass-fed meats than processed foods that travel thousands of miles to get to your plate.

Celeste: Is there anything else you'd like to add?

Jackie: We usually have people stay for a night, sometimes two. Europeans often stay the longest, perhaps two weeks. They often only leave the property once or twice to go shopping for essentials that we don't have here, and then settle in to enjoy the peace and tranquility. Besides the diversity of meats and vegetables we provide here on our farm our entire region is filled with an amazing variety of fresh local foods. People can walk right from our farm up to Alyson's Orchard, an orchard which grows almost 200 different varieties of fruit. So they can really go for days without having to get in their cars. That's a very special and unique thing and very empowering for folks. We encourage our guests to compost, too.

In our community, besides our grass-fed meat and the neighbor's fruit, we also have access to raw milk, talented artisan bread bakers, a winery, ice cream made with local cow milk, cheese makers, and maple syrup and honey producers. So lots of our guests bring a cooler and stock up on foods from us as well as farms all around us. Then they bring it home and still eat well for a while.

Innovative and Holistic Farmer, Dan Kittredge

Dan Kittredge, from North Brookfield, MA is on a mission. He has a phenomenal understanding of how plants live and thrive. He feels that current agricultural practices often work against these basic natural relationships to the detriment of our health. Dan and his organization, the Bionutrient Food Association, are determined to "create health from the soil up."

Celeste: What is the mission of the Bionutrient Food Association?

Dan: The mission of the BFA is to increase the quality of the food supply. Our first core constituency is the growers of food. We want to educate growers about the logistics of creating healthier plants, greater yields and reduced production costs. Our second core constituency is the eaters of food. People who understand the full ramifications of higher quality food on their health will make their pocketbook decisions accordingly. Our third core constituency is the purveyors of food. We want to help retailers determine the quality of food before they purchase it for better flavor and longer shelf life.

Our analyses show—across the board—that people in this country have large mineral deficiencies compared to people eighty years ago. Not only does remineralization correlate to more nutrition, better taste and longer shelf life but it also correlates to the environment. We are interested in more carbon sequestration (getting some of the excess carbon out of our air and back into our soil through the plants). This will hopefully help to rebalance weather patterns.

Celeste: So the environment would be greatly enhanced if we improved our soils?

Dan: Most farmers add nitrogen to the soil because they don't think that plants can harvest nitrogen from the atmosphere. Yet, for millions of years, plants have been doing just that. So, we don't need to apply nitrogen. Not only does this create pollutants in the runoff, but it gives money to the chemical companies. I believe that if plants are healthy, they are indigestible to bacteria and fungi (which is key to defining healthy plants). You also don't need pesticides or fungicides or all those toxic chemicals. If you have people eating healthy food, their physiology is working well and most have no need for pharmaceuticals. Then there is less money going to these corporations that are flourishing on disease. So we are focusing on food quality.

Celeste: When did the BFA start?

Dan: We became a nonprofit organization in February of 2012.

Celeste: What would you advise folks who are beginners—who maybe want to plant a few things in the backyard—to put in their soil right away?

Dan: It's hard to say when you don't know what's missing. A soil test could tell you what you need. Kelp is always good because it is high in trace minerals. Alfalfa meal (not GMO) would also be okay because it provides food for the worms. In non-arid areas, sea salt can be applied at two pounds per 1,000 square feet. The best idea, though, is to have the soil tested so that you know what's missing.

I'm a big fan of hay mulch. I keep the soil around all my crops covered. The mulch is the food for the living soil organisms and the earthworms. When the earthworms kick into gear, then you are all set. They will balance everything out. They will take care of your soil for you. So you want to create a reality where the earthworms are going to flourish. Irrigation is also really important.

Celeste: What do you like to mulch with?

Dan: I use the least expensive thing which is available to me and that is mulch hay. If I was closer to the ocean, I would certainly use kelp. Some people use straw which is generally more expensive than hay.

> The amount of weeding that I do on my farm is almost none at all.

Celeste: Don't you get a lot of seeds with the hay?

Dan: The amount of weeding that I do on my farm is almost none at all. I think it's because I don't till the soil. Therefore, I have a fungal community established in the soil. This is truly as close to nature as it gets. I believe that the plants that we call crops prefer a fungal-dominated ecosystem in the soil. The plants that we call weeds prefer a bacterially-dominated ecosystem. So when you till the soil, you shred the fungal hyphae (thread-like organisms) and the bacteria become dominant and the bacterial metabolites are the preferred food for weeds. Weeds have a job in nature which is to cover soil. Nature does not like bare soil. You don't see bare soil anywhere in nature except where the soil is totally depleted.

Celeste: So you don't turn over your soil?

Dan: If I have sod and I want a garden, I will turn it over. However, once the beds are established, I will do a shallow till if I want to plant a seedbed. The less destruction to the structure, the better. My earthworms take care of aerating the soil. If you have a good earthworm population, they're going up and down and all over the place. Thirty earthworms per square yard will till your soil nine times in a year. You should be able to reach down in your soil and bring up a handful. That's a good sign of looseness. If you've got that, there's no reason to till. Tillage is actually very disruptive to soil life. Depending on the size of your area, tilling can kill off many, many organisms. Because the bacteria and fungi in the soil are helping to feed the plants, killing off these organisms is counterproductive. Nature has evolved where the bacteria and fungi aid in feeding the plants. A lot of the things that we do in agriculture are ineffectual and unwise. That's why we have weak plants susceptible to disease and pests.

> Thirty earthworms per square yard will till your soil nine times in a year.

Celeste: I have permanent beds so I never walk on them, but I have been using a broad fork to loosen the soil.

Dan: That's a good thing to do. Opening up the soil is important. Wherever you don't have air, the soil life can't breathe. Where the soil life can't breathe, the plant can't be fed. Air is massively important. Air is a critical piece of the puzzle. Water is also a critical piece of the puzzle. Keeping the soil moist should be an even higher priority than getting the soil tested and fixing mineral deficiencies. If the soil isn't kept moist, all the organisms that live there die of thirst. So it doesn't matter what minerals are there; the feeders of the plants are gone.

Celeste: This was a problem for me because the ledge is so close to the surface, it's easy for my garden to dry out.

Dan: Then prioritize a drip tape. It's pretty easy to automate a system. It runs from a hose and can have an on/off timer attached. I transplant, put the drip tape down and mulch and I am done. After this, there is very little work to do. I work on my farm about twenty hours a week and sell about $1,000 worth of vegetables each week on about 1/2 acre of land.

Celeste: That's pretty good!

Dan: That's called lazy farming. If you do it right—if you understand what the soil life needs to function well and you can give it those things—you can sit back and do very little. Plants have evolved a symbiotic relationship with soil life. The soil life is actually helping to feed them not simple ions but complex compounds. The plants are placing sugars with amino acids attached to them into the soil to feed the soil life and the soil life is feeding back up these complex compounds which the plants use to build up their bodies.

> I work on my farm about twenty hours a week and sell about $1,000 worth of vegetables each week on about 1/2 acre of land.

Celeste: What makes your organization different from others?

Dan: Current organic certifications focus on what the farmers are giving their crops instead of how nutritious the crops themselves are as the objective. We feel it is necessary to focus more on the quality of the food that people are actually going to eat than what the farmers give their soil.

If you would like more information on the BFA or Dan's farming practices, visit his website at bionutrient.org.

A Truly Holistic Meat Farmer, Chris Caserta

Chris and Caitlin Caserta run "Walpole Valley Farms," a gorgeous 100-acre farm in Walpole, NH. Chris went to Joel Salatin's two-day Intensive Discovery Seminar in 2007 and uses much the same methods for enhancing the well-being not only of his livestock but also of his land. I had a conversation with him recently.

Celeste: You have an interesting way of farming. It's a little bit different than the traditional way. Could you explain it to me?

Chris: First of all, we're a diversified farm (Walpole Valley Farms). Most large farms do one thing; they're chicken farmers or pig farmers or whatever. We have two types of chickens (layers and broilers), pigs, cows, turkeys and sheep. Being diversified helps us financially. Right now beef is relatively pricey so the other meats are selling better. Pork and chicken are doing quite well currently. We're also different because we strive to put back into the land as much as we're taking out. That's one of the biggest misconceptions our nation faces. People use fertilizer, but replacing nutrients is not just about

> We're also different because we strive to put back into the land as much as we're taking out.

NPK (nitrogen, phosphorus and potassium), it's about animal manure and hoof impact. We give back to the land by moving animals around often and in symbiosis with each other. Another way that our farm is different from most other farms is that we not only let the animals express themselves (such as letting pigs romp and forage in the forest), but we let the land express itself as well. Certain times of the year, we just let the grass grow in the fields. We don't care if it reseeds itself. We trample it with the cows. Their hooves aerate the ground and push plant matter into the soil for fertilization. It also lays the grass down on the ground, providing shade shelter and moisture so that new grass can grow.

The traditional method of haying is called twelve to two. Farmers cut when it is twelve inches high and leave two inches on the ground.

The traditional method of haying is called twelve to two. Farmers cut when it is twelve inches high and leave two inches on the ground. For a hay field, this method might be all the field ever sees. It just so happens that timothy, orchard grass and clovers thrive in that environment. However, there could be other seeds in there that are a thousand years old and would pop up if given the chance.

Celeste: So how often do you move the cows?

Chris: It depends on the time of year. With cows, it's a minimum of once a day and as much as three times a day. Certain times of the day are the most advantageous. For example, when the old-timers cut their hay, they would do it in the late afternoon of a sunny day. That's when the energy of the plant is coming up out of the ground and going to the outermost reaches of the plant in order to harvest the solar energy. On a cloudy day, that doesn't happen. The energy stays in the roots.

We used to take care of the chicken layers first thing in the morning and then we would take care of the cows. But first thing in the morning, there is less nutrition in the plants. However, the cows would eat them because they were hungry. Now we move them so that they eat more in the late afternoon. In the summer, cows will usually eat between 9:00am and 11:00am before it gets too hot. Then they'll lounge in the early afternoon. After that, they'll go and eat again for quite a while, sometimes even after it gets dark.

Celeste: So you move the chickens first?

Chris: We move the laying hens every three to seven days depending on the weather and how much food is available in that specific spot. They're in a much larger spot than the broilers and it takes them a while to fertilize the whole area.

Celeste: What do they eat?

Chris: The first thing that the chickens usually eat is animal protein. They love worms, grasshoppers and crickets. Those are big protein meals for them and they also eat a lot of small stuff that we can hardly see. They're getting some grain so they have those carbohydrate needs met, but they are hardcore omnivores and related to birds of prey. If the land is well-managed, there's a plethora of food choices for them to eat. That's why we don't use chemical fertilizers. It makes the grass grow great and green, but eventually kills off many microorganisms. The broiler chickens we move every day no matter what. Chicken tractors work great because they can be moved daily to hit every square bit of ground which is more sanitary for the chickens.

Celeste: So chickens are giving to the soil because of the chicken poop?

Chris: What they are leaving behind is fresh chicken manure which is very effective in feeding the pasture at the right concentration. If it's too high a concentration, it can burn the ground. A good concentration works out to be 200 pounds of nitrogen per acre. You can actually see the improvement in the lush, green fields.

Celeste: And when do the cows come into these fields?

Chris: The cows come in at various times. Think about that hay scenario— you want something similar. If the grass is too short, the cows are not getting the full benefit of the solar energy. Once the grasses are at least four to five inches high, the cows are really reaping the benefit of that solar energy. After the plants get really tall, they start sending their nutrients back to their roots and go to seed. We don't fuss too much about this, though, because if it happens to be a little bit late, we get the benefit of lots of seedlings. We have the cows trample it completely.

> After the plants get really tall, they start sending their nutrients back to their roots and go to seed.

151

Celeste: Why do you want the cows to trample it?

Chris: Trampling is not wasting. It's creating more organic matter for the soil. What you don't want is bare ground.

Farmers' Market Organizer, Jill Robinson

Jill Robinson is a spunky, dedicated organizer who was instrumental in setting up a farmers' market where she lives in Walpole, NH.

Celeste: What kind of process did you go through to set up the Walpole Farmers' Market?

Jill: I knew some of the veggie farmers and meat farmers whose products I had bought at their farms. Some other residents and I had a big energy fair in Walpole, NH several years ago and we thought that we could make the farmers' market part of this fair. These farmers that I knew then told me about the other farmers in town and I called them. There ended up being twelve or fifteen in our small town of 4,000. The farmers' market was a big success at the energy fair. The farmers loved it and the shoppers loved it. Soon, folks began saying, "I wonder if we should have a permanent market?" So at the next town meeting we took a survey. We caught people on their way in and asked them if they would like to have a farmers' market and most said that they would. We then put the word out to the farmers. However, initially we only had three people commit to setting up a market every single week. The idea was a bit scary and others thought it might not work because it was new. But, once we had these three people committed to coming every week, the others began saying, "Okay, I'll try that too."

Fortunately for us, a couple of the farmers had been involved in farmers' markets elsewhere, one for over thirty years. So he knew a lot about what could go wrong. When we wrote up our guidelines, we knew what we needed to include to avoid those pitfalls. We put our guidelines up on the Walpole Farmers' Market website so that everything was transparent. Anyone who wanted the information could go and look it up. That's how it started.

Celeste: What kind of rules do you have in your guidelines?

Jill: Our mission is to support local agriculture and sustainable practices. Guidelines include information about what can be sold. For instance, people can only sell items that they grow or produce. You can't sell somebody else's harvest. In farmers' markets where they allow that, the misuse is astonishing. Folks would go to large supermarkets, buy wilted old produce and resell it. We wanted to avoid that. We wanted to have real farmers who could give shoppers complete information about what they were buying. The guidelines also include details like putting prices on your offerings so that people don't have to ask you how much something costs. People are very reluctant to ask because they get a little embarrassed. A full list of the guidelines can be viewed on the Market Admin page of walpolefarmersmarket.com.

> We wanted to have real farmers who could give shoppers complete information about what they were buying.

Celeste: What have been the best and worst parts of the farmers' market?

Jill: The best parts are easy access to very high-quality food, the community feeling and that it's held in a pleasant location. Families can come with little children and it's safe to let them run around. People like it as a community event. The worst part is that our small town doesn't have enough people interested in local food to make it profitable for the farmers. So, every year we go ask whether it is worth continuing the market. Nobody wants to give it up because it's a nice community event. But from a strictly financial viewpoint, the farmers could be using their time to greater advantage if they were home on the farm. I think that there's some magic population number that supports a market. In Walpole, NH, a town of 4,000 people, we don't adequately support a market. In the city of Keene, NH, with a population of 23,500, there is a thriving market.

Celeste: So you need a pretty good-sized population to support a market?

> # I think it's a good investment in the future and I think that's why these farmers hang in there.

Jill: Or a population that is more concerned with what they eat. We're only at the beginning of the "Just Eat Real Food" movement. More and more people are realizing that what they eat and their health are closely linked. Podcasts like Underground Wellness (http://undergroundwellness.com/radio/), and so many others are helping us understand the link between vibrant wellness and the clean, local, nutrient-dense food that is available at farmers' markets. Another organization that has an abundance of good information can be found here: slowfoodusa.org.

Hopefully, our farmers' market can last until we get enough momentum behind us. I think it's a good investment in the future and I think that's why these farmers hang in there. They wouldn't be farmers unless they were interested in investing in the future to begin with. You have to have a serious commitment to the future to be a farmer. Keeping the farmers' market going is a part of that commitment.

Nutritional Advisor, Sandra Littell

Sandra Littell is a nutritional counselor. She is a Chapter Leader for the Weston A. Price Foundation (an organization dedicated to educating people about real food), has studied with Dr. Natasha Campbell-McBride (GAPS—Gut And Psychology Syndrome*), a member of the Nutritional Therapy Association and is extremely knowledgeable on specific nutrients and what they do in the body. She is currently working on a cookbook and, I must say, everything that she has cooked for me has been exquisite.

Celeste: What got you into the nutritional field?

Sandra: I was dealing with serious health issues within my family that I sensed were nutritionally related. A friend steered me to Dr. Price's work. Maybe I thought I knew what good nutrition was because I read all the latest health recommendations, but something was up when my children and I still had lots of nagging issues. Dr. Price inspired me to look at nutrition in a new way.

Celeste: What basically did you get from Dr. Price's book?

Sandra: He did a really phenomenal thing. He wanted to understand what the basics of human nutrition and healing were, so he studied people around the world who had that optimal health generation after generation. He studied fourteen different groups around the world who had not been touched by western food, "the displacing food of commerce." His findings started me on my path. I studied on my own for years, and eventually became a GAPS practitioner. I've been practicing this type of nutrition with my own family for several years and the results have spoken for themselves. My kids all got healthy and will attest to it. I had lots of little things which—looking back— were much bigger than I realized. I nipped a lot of serious problems in the bud. I've never had more energy or felt so emotionally stable.

Celeste: What do you see as the most common mistakes that people make in their diets?

Sandra: The most common mistake that I see is people trusting the main media for their nutritional information and not understanding that the American Diabetes Association is partially funded by the Sugar Association or that the American Heart Association is partially funded by proponents of the cholesterol theory. People need to understand that these supposed philanthropic organizations are biased. They are looking to push their products. Sugar is huge in our country. It's in many, many products. Processed fats are also huge in this country—they are very profitable for the food industry. These processed fats have been altered so that they have become a nonfood, great for business because they are very shelf stable and can last forever but very debilitating for our bodies. Every one of our cells depends on a healthy, real fat. The foundational vitamins, A, D, E and K are very important for our health. Vitamin A and vitamin D work together; it's not good to take either one alone. They are in a natural balance to each other in wholesome foods such as (pasture-raised) egg yolks, (wild-caught) seafood and roe, raw milk (from grass-fed cows and goats) and are especially rich in fermented cod liver or skate oil. Without adequate amounts of these fat-soluble vitamins, our cells cannot be healthy! Thus, all the other necessary nutrients such as minerals, proteins, and water-soluble vitamins like vitamin C cannot be properly absorbed!

Celeste: What are the best fats to use?

Sandra: The real ones; the ones our forefathers used (before we purchased food in boxes). Butter, cream, raw whole milk (only from healthy animals) as well as naturally rendered beef tallow, lamb tallow, palm oil and coconut oil are real fats. Fats that are safe to cook with are the ones that are most stable at room temperature without hydrogenation. Folks often like to use olive oil, but it is really not as stable as the others. Olive oil is great if it really is olive oil and not doctored with a cheaper oil like many of the ones that are bottled in Italy. It's best for drizzling on food after it is cooked. The three things I try to steer people away from are refined sugar, refined salt and doctored fats.

> Fats that are safe to cook with are the ones that are most stable at room temperature without hydrogenation.

Celeste: What kinds of foods do you recommend?

Sandra: The best foods are biodynamically,** organically grown, whole fruits and vegetables in season, or canned if not in season, and meats and fats from healthily-raised (know your farmer) local, pastured animals (not grain-fed). If you can, it's best to know the health of the soil upon which the animals are grazing and that grows your food. There was a study done in Rio De Janeiro in 1992 presented at the Earth Summit Conference about the loss of minerals in soils around the world. In Africa, there was a seventy percent loss of minerals. In North America, there was an eighty-six percent loss—back in 1992. Minerals are the spark plugs of life. We can't live without enzymes but enzymes can't function without minerals. So, it's critically important to get proper minerals and there are many more than the NPK (nitrogen, phosphorus and potassium) that we've been putting into soil for our crops.

Celeste: Anything else you want to add?

Sandra: I think it's really fun teaching people about true nutrition because most peoples' perception of healthy food is that it is bland and doesn't taste good. When you eat properly-raised food, it is extremely delicious and also very satisfying. Your cravings melt away, moods stabilize, your attention improves, your skin improves, your immunity improves and your physical stamina improves. That's what I've witnessed with myself, my kids and my clients. I also teach fermenting because that process increases the nutrient content of foods. Turning cabbage into sauerkraut increases the bioavailability of the vitamin C ten times. And, you can ferment almost anything. Fermented foods also contain digestive enzymes and probiotics. We are a nation consuming too many antibiotics from our commonly over-prescribed treatments as well as in conventionally-raised animal products such as meat and milk. These antibiotics kill the healthy bacteria as well as the pathogenic ones. We need to replace the healthy ones in order to have a healthy gut.

> **Minerals are the spark plugs of life. We can't live without enzymes but enzymes can't function without minerals.**

Celeste: Isn't that the basis of the GAPS diet?

Sandra: Yes. If you aren't digesting your food into small enough particles for your cells to actually use, your organs cannot perform their functions adequately.

Dr. Campbell-McBride believes (as did Hippocrates) that all illnesses begin in the gut. Her website is full of pertinent information and can be found at gaps.me.

Information on the Weston A. Price Foundation can be found here: westonaprice.org.

***Biodynamics is a system of farming that goes above and beyond most current practices. It was first developed in the 1920s based on the spiritual insights and practical suggestions of Dr. Rudolf Steiner. It's also a movement for new thinking and practices in all aspects of life connected to food and agriculture. More information can be found at biodynamics.com.*

Beekeeper, Jodi Turner

Jodi Turner and her husband, Dean, teach beekeeping at their home in Swanzey, NH. They are both quite concerned about the decline in the bee population and are eager to spread the word about their dwindling numbers. They want people to know what products to avoid purchasing in order to save the bees.

Celeste: What got you into beekeeping?

Jodi: I was working at Stonewall Farm (a teaching farm in Keene, NH) and they offered classes on beekeeping for free. I thought it would be kind of cool to sit in. I wasn't going to be a beekeeper. I wasn't going to spend any money. I wasn't going to do anything except watch. I thought it would be interesting because, when I was about ten years old, I went to the Friendly Farm (a child-oriented petting farm in NH). They had an observation hive there. I remember watching this thing of bees with glass. I thought it was so amazing that I didn't get stung; how can that be? Where do they go? I had so many questions.

After I took the class, I was intrigued and thought "I'm going to learn how to keep bees." And I did. But now it has become something larger. I absolutely adore everything about bees. I honestly can't imagine life without them.

> Every third bite of food that you take has been touched by a pollinator.

Celeste: Because they are essential to our survival?

Jodi: They are. Every third bite of food that you take has been touched by a pollinator. Honeybees are the biggest pollinators. If we didn't have honeybees, we wouldn't have a lot of the foods that we eat. We take it for granted, but if the bee population continues to decline, the work that these amazing creatures do could end. If so, we would need to pollinate our crops ourselves. I've seen videos where people pollinate with feathers. "You can do this yourself! You can pollinate your own garden!" I'm thinking "We are crazy." It seems crazy to me. We already have these beautiful, amazing creatures that pollinate for us. We give them something; they give us something and it's a great partnership. That's what my husband and my company's slogan (Imagine that—honey!) is all about: the partnership.

Celeste: So why are bees in trouble?

Jodi: That depends on who you talk to. I think that it has a lot to do with pesticides. CCD (Colony Collapse Disorder) really came about in 2006 when neonicotinoids (neonics) came on the market. Neonicotinoid ingredients include: acetamiprid, clothianidin, dinotefuran, imidacloprid, Nitenpyram, Thiacloprid and Thiamethoxam. Before buying an insecticide, check for these ingredients. They are in dozens, if not more, of insecticides.

Author's note: *I went on the internet and found these ingredients in many products including the following: Advantage (flea killer for pets), Admire, Aloft , Bifenthrin, Bithor, Confidor, Conguard, Coretect, Dominion, Flagship, Gaucho, I Maxx Pro, Ima-Jet, Imicide, Imida-Teb, ImidaPro, ImGold, Marathon, Meridian, Merit, Nuprid, Optigard, Optrol, Premise, Prothor, Provado, Temprid, Triple Crown Insecticide, Turfthor and Xytect. These products are currently used to kill other, troublesome insects but they are also killing the bees. Neonicotinoids are currently banned in Europe.*

Neonicotinoids affect the neurological system of bees and other insects. The bees that have been infected come into the hives and as they rub against each other (that's how they communicate), they spread this disease. An infected bee goes out and they can't remember how to get back. It's a neurological thing. So once all the foragers are gone, the young bees and the queen are left on their own. Ninety-nine percent of the bees are gone from that one hive. It's scary. I haven't personally had this happen to my hives. Perhaps that's because here in New Hampshire, there is less monocropping (planting many acres of one crop) and pesticide use.

Celeste: And that's another problem—the monocropping—that makes it a food desert for the bees.

Jodi: Totally. And the fertilizers, fungicides, herbicides, or whatever the farmers are using, all go into the soil. Many farmers are fertilizing the ground with chemicals which will eventually cause the soil to lose all of its nutrients. We get rid of all those weeds, but what are we really doing? We have to look at the big picture.

We have to remember, too, that the big seed companies now have control over most of the seeds. And, a lot of these seeds already have pesticides on them. The big box stores all over the country are probably not even aware that they are selling seeds and plants that are full of toxins.

Celeste: So what can we do to help?

Jodi: I teach beekeeping. I started out as a beekeeper but now I feel like a pied piper. I am spreading the word about environmental consciousness. Every beekeeper that we bring in now thinks about what they are putting on their lawn, what their neighbors are putting on their lawns and what is going on in the world. Before becoming a beekeeper, they probably didn't think about the environment in this way. By teaching, we are educating. People often listen without hearing. I can't tell you how many people I talk to that tell me they are hearing about the need to pay more attention to the environment for the first time.

> Every beekeeper that we bring in now thinks about what they are putting on their lawn, what their neighbors are putting on their lawns and what is going on in the world.

Celeste: People are starting to pay attention which is a good thing.

Jodi: Twenty years ago I thought that the word "organic" was hippy-dippy because I was totally mainstream. My thought processes since have really changed. We need to pay attention to what we are using in our yards. What about growing clover or some other plant that will stay green all summer long even if not watered (instead of grass)? What about planting flowers that will attract pollinators?

Another thing that my husband, Dean, and I are doing (besides writing a book)—is setting up a pollinator garden called the "Northeast Honey Bee Sanctuary." We want to teach young kids about what is going on. Maybe they, in turn, will teach their parents.

Celeste: And planting different kinds of flowers that bloom at different times of the year would help the bees

by providing them with food over the entire summer season.

Jodi: Totally!

Celeste: Anything else that you would like to add?

Jodi: Yes, everyone should think about having a garden.

When I was little, my Dad had a garden that was only about fifteen feet by ten feet, but it was huge to me. We had all kinds of vegetables in that garden and that was what we ate. It doesn't need to be a huge space; it can be plants on a patio.

Also, I have ten hives in my backyard but I hardly ever see the bees. They go out and forage then they come back. They are not a bother to me at all.

> I have ten hives in my backyard but I hardly ever see the bees. They go out and forage then they come back. They are not a bother to me at all.

Author's note:
Alternative to flea collars. For decades, Bob and I have been giving our cats and dogs one heaping tablespoon of brewer's yeast (nutritional yeast) with their meals all year long. We don't use commercial products and we have never noticed a single flea.

Renewable Energy Merchant, Pablo Fleischmann

It's lovely to get electric bills in the neighborhood of $5 most months of the year.

Pablo Fleischmann and Valerie Piedmont own Green Energy Options, a renewable energy store in downtown Keene, NH. Several years ago they installed a photovoltaic system, including battery back-up, at our home. Bob and I have been very happy with this system; it's lovely to get electric bills in the neighborhood of $5 most months of the year. Also, when the grid goes down, the electricity flows into the batteries so quickly that the clocks don't even blink. I spoke with Pablo to see how the solar industry is doing today.

Celeste: How did you become interested in renewable resources?

Pablo: I've always had a tangential interest but, the truth is, I met Valerie, a woman who in her prior existence was a nuclear protester. She was not going to have anything to do with feeding into the grid, so we lived without running water or refrigeration for seven years. The solar came about by me saying, "You know, honey, we could have lights instead of kerosene lamps." I opened up a book, accumulated the pieces and I put together our own electrical system. Nowadays, the majority of solar has no batteries which means less pieces; it's a simple grid-tie. When the Sun is shining, it powers the house and any extra power goes into the grid. If the grid goes down, the electricity stops.

Celeste: Who are your primary customers?

Pablo: Most of the people who do solar are either empty nesters or people who are retired or are approaching retirement. They see the future (perhaps with rising energy costs) and they want to lock in their costs, or, they finally have the money to spend. Many people have always known it's the right thing to do and now they have the opportunity.

Celeste: What does your store sell?

Pablo: We began the business in 2007 with the primary idea of selling solar electric and solar water. We are still a renewable energy store, but now about fifty percent of our business is selling wood and pellet stoves. Solar here in New Hampshire has slowed down. We're doing larger systems, but fewer of them. Most photovoltaic systems are a simple grid-tie where, if the grid goes down, everything goes down. That is the cheapest way to go. However, some of the population wants the independence and the security of knowing that their systems will still work during a power outage. Many folks around here have no woodstoves so their heat—even if it's a Rinnai (popular gas heating) system—depends upon electricity.

Celeste: What should people know before incorporating solar?

Pablo: In terms of an investment, a simple grid-tie is the way to go. This is a system that uses solar power when the Sun is shining, but remains locked into the grid for when it is not. If you generate more power than you use on sunny days, the energy goes into the grid and your meter runs backwards.

> In terms of an investment, a simple grid tie is the way to go.

Celeste: What about government programs?

Pablo: There are still government programs available for tax credit but they vary from state to state in terms of solar electric and solar hot water. The federal government began offering a tax credit in 2005. That credit, as it exists now, is set to expire at the end of 2016 but it will probably be around, just in another form, after 2016. Right now it's a thirty percent tax credit. Some utilities also have rebates.

Celeste: Anything else you'd like to add?

Pablo: It's amazing how many people come into our store and say that one of these days, we'll figure out that as a country, population or race, it's important

for a sustainable future to look at renewables. Sustainable energy should be incorporated more into our infrastructure. Because I'm a business, I have to explain to people why it makes sense financially. In New Hampshire, a simple grid-tie system will pay for itself in ten to eleven years. In Massachusetts, it's half of that time (because different states offer separate rebate programs and have other policies that affect it.) If you would like to see the ones in your state, go to dsireusa.org. (Database of State Incentives for Renewables and Efficiency).

Chapter Thirteen

Conclusion

Everything that we touch carries the vibration of how we have touched it. All that comes to us from others carries the vibrations of how they have touched it. That is why it is so important to be gentle and kind with our plants and animals, to love and care for the piece of Earth that we walk. It matters.

It may sometimes feel as if we have very little power over what happens on this planet. Nothing could be further from the truth. Every single thing that we do is like a rock thrown into a pond; it ripples out forever. How we choose to spend our dollars is extremely important. We need to think globally, but act locally. It is a national security issue to be able to feed ourselves from within our own communities. If we don't have the space to grow and raise our own food, we need to support the local farmers who do.

Big agribusiness is not good for us or our planet. They have made food deserts for our bees. They have made conditions where more and more toxic sprays are necessary to grow our vegetables. Animals are now raised in conditions that are deplorable and fed foods that are difficult, if not impossible, for them to digest. But, people are beginning to understand.

According to an October 2, 2012 article in the Washington Post by Brad Plummer, the US farm count rose by four percent between 2002 and 2007, the very first time since 1940 that the number of small farms in this country increased. Farmers' Markets are appearing left and right in small towns and big cities alike. CSAs (Community Supported Agriculture) are growing. But they need our support. Find a way to work with them. Some farmers will trade goods for labor. Consider getting together with friends and neighbors for some group buying at a discount. In-season vegetables and fruits can be had for a bargain if you purchase a large amount (and how lovely it is to pull these out of the freezer or pantry in the winter!). Freezers cost very little to run and can be located on sheltered porches or outbuildings (but not frost-free ones). Learn how to use everything that you buy (bone broths are especially important to our health).

If you can't afford to purchase all organic produce, start with buying those that would typically contain the most pesticides. Potatoes, apples, grapes, summer squash, kale, spinach, sweet peppers and lettuce are among the "dirtiest." Asparagus, avocados, sweet potatoes, cabbage, mushrooms, eggplant and onions have the fewest pesticides or herbicides (as of this writing). This list is always changing, though, and a current one can usually be found at www.ewg. org/foodnews.

If you do decide to try your hand at gardening, start small. What is your favorite vegetable? Begin there. Local nurseries are full of individuals who are not only knowledgeable, but want to help. And it's vitally important to shop at these local establishments. Big box stores may have plants and potting soils for less money but you run the risk of importing new bugs and diseases onto your property.

We not only can, but we **do** make a difference. Be part of the solution. It's not that hard, really, just a matter of making thoughtful choices.

Index

U

Umbelliferae, 24
Underground Wellness, 154
University of Mississippi, 132
University of New Hampshire, 133
USDA, 137

V

vitamins, 49, 71, 92, 93, 105, 111,
    155, 156, 157

W

Walpole, NH, 126, 133, 135, 139,
    149, 152
Walpole Farmers' Market, 133, 152
Walpole Valley Farms, 139-144, 149
wasps, 107-108
water, garden, 12, 26, 40, 121, 127-
    129
water, solar, 163-165
water system, 127-129, 148
water system, grey, 13-14, 121
water-bath canner, 96-97
weeding, 40, 146
Weston A. Price Foundation, 154,
    158
whey recipe, 101
Whippie, Rebecca, 137
white fish sauce recipe, 91
Wightman, Tim, 122-125
www.biodynamics.com, 158
www.bionutrients.org, 148
www.dsireusa.org, 165
www.ewg.org/foodnews/, 167
www.farmstayus.org, 139, 141
www.innatvalleyfarms.com, 139
www.jmgkids.us/, 139
www.slowfoodusa.org, 154
www.solarcookers.org, 121
www.undergroundwellness.com, 154
www.walpolefarmersmarket.com,
    153
www.westonaprice.org, 158

Z

Zachary, Nick, 126-129
zucchini, 34, 35, 47, 48
zucchini flower recipe, 50-51

Recipes